FINDING REVENUE

FINDING REVENUE

HOW FOUNDERS, OWNERS, AND CEOS LEAD MARKETING AND SALES

R J KROON

For Jim Goughenour, my intellectually-gifted, adventurous and courageous colleague, supporter, mentor, advisor, avid-business-book-reviewer, and 40-year friend.

CONTENTS

ACKNOWLEDGMENTS

This book would not have been possible without the support and encouragement of my wife Melinda Dunnihoo. She lived through many of the career stories that are part of the book and encouraged me to write about my experiences.

If you are the spouse of a CEO, Owner, or Founder, you often find yourself 'on stage' alongside your partner. This is particularly true in smaller communities where you interact with others from your company in churches, schools, restaurants, civic organizations, and sometimes on the street in your neighborhood. Unless you have experienced this, you may not appreciate the burden of always being an example.

In my career, we were also blessed to travel to Europe and Asia several times with company colleagues and hundreds of customers. We had times where several days in a row we were interacting with customers every waking moment. My wife was a clear asset in these situations and a partner that deserves credit for my success.

My editor, Shannan Saunders, has clearly made the manuscript a better work. I appreciate the quality level she expects and her attention to detail. She has been professional, responsive, thorough, and patient. She has also been a great resource beyond editing as her experience and network bring additional value.

Dave Zauhar from Z Squared Design is responsible for bringing the power of graphic art to this book. His contributions add the visual sizzle. He combines serious thought and relevance with playful, fun designs. There are stories to tell about every graphic.

The effort to produce this book began with Claudia Loens at Wordflirt. I began writing a few blog posts for her, then a few more. At one point, we agreed "these should be a book". And apparently, they are.

INTRODUCTION

Monday, September 12, 1988, 8:15am

My wife answered the phone.

"Hi, this is Cindy. Is Bob there?"

My wife, "He's on his way."

"Ok, Dan wants to see him when he gets into the office."

My wife, "Ah ... No ... he's on his way... *to Seattle.*"

This phone call occurred on my first day as a general manager. Dan was my boss for only the previous two weeks. I did not bother to tell him I was taking another position in the corporation. I also did not expect anyone would try to call me at home.

Let me explain.

This story starts with events nine months earlier. In January of 1988, I became assistant to the president of the corporation.

Others did not know my real role, and I saw no upside to telling anyone. Rod told me I could help him with special projects and raise my hand if I saw a general management position I liked. There was no rush, and I had no obligation to take the first opening that occurred.

I was fortunate, Rod was a great mentor and I had the opportunity to become quickly involved in high-level, strategically important projects.

I passed on the first two opportunities but was quite interested in the third, which came up in late summer; division president for a small division of the corporation with a headquarters located in Seattle. It was a turnaround situation and I was involved in developing a turnaround plan. I knew that the execution of the plan was workable and would succeed.

There were other attractive features of the opportunity. Compared to most others, this position offered the broadest spectrum of responsibility. I would manage my own factories, sales force, marketing, human resources, accounting, and physical distribution. Finally, most of the other general management opportunities in the corporation were more limited in scope.

Importantly, the position was on the West Coast. By written policy, the company airplane based in the Midwest was not to be used to travel west of the Rockies. I would have minimal help from corporate as the travel would be a consideration.

On the other hand, I also knew that to make this succeed politically, I would need an advocate at the home office. My boss, president of the corporation and my mentor, was a perfect fit.

I raised my hand and accepted the offer for the position.

Then trouble came to the plan.

When Rod became president of the corporation in addition to being president of the largest division, he did not move his office to the corporate headquarters as expected, instead remaining in the offices of the largest division. This was an unusual decision and it was taking months to hire someone to be the president of the division. There was no alignment in thinking between my boss and his boss, the Chairman of the Board, Stan.

A week or so after I had accepted the position in Seattle, Rod announced he was taking a job as president of another company. Now there were two top leadership vacuums in the company. I lost my corporate advocate.

Rod had a candidate he was advocating to replace himself as president of the most significant division, but the chairman, Stan, did not agree to hire the candidate.

I can only guess as to the possible root cause of the disagreement; Rod's candidate was sales and marketing oriented and Stan wanted someone with an engineering background.

Over the weekend following Rod's departure announcement, the Chairman lurched into action and hired someone with an engineering background. Dan.

Who was this person? After learning a bit about his background, I realized I could reach out to a friend who had worked in Dan's earlier company. In other words, I did a reference check.

The call was quite clear, "*... Are you s#!~ing me? Did they hire Dan? I would never ...*"

A vice president in the division, Ned, my boss a year earlier, also did his diligence. When we compared each other's notes, we ultimately agreed.

I was in a tricky situation. Should I stay to work for the new division president or get out of town knowing I had no advocate at corporate? I reneged on the new position.

Dan showed up a few days later, and he exactly lived up to the expectations I had from my reference check.

Meanwhile, Rod was still around and still working on the transition.

He convinced Stan to hire two people, Dan, and his candidate, Larry. Dan would be the president of the largest division and Larry would serve as a group vice president with the job in Seattle and other small divisions reporting to him.

Larry showed up a few days later, and he lived up to the expectations I learned from Rod, in a positive way.

The position in Seattle was still open, so I asked exiting-Rod if I could un-renege and could take the job. Could he help me?

On a Thursday, I met with Larry. Friday, we laid out the plans for an agenda and travel. I bought plane tickets and went home for the weekend.

I guess nobody told Dan. On the other hand, maybe they did.

The Takeaway

Emotions, politics, and reactionary decisions play a significant role when filling top leadership positions. Some would argue that emotions are a part of every decision in business. Top leadership choices are not exempt.

All big decisions have risk. You must assess both the upside and the downside to your choices. There are very seldom clear-cut answers to your dilemmas. In the absence of concrete evidence, many decisions evolve from emotion; what you feel is the best decision?

You may think you have a well laid out plan for your career or your business, but events that are out of your control impact outcomes. You do not work in a vacuum. Relationships can be fragile and what you believe you have today might not be there tomorrow.

Success or Failure

Did I have misgivings about my chances for success in the new assignment? I knew I needed a mentor. I had a fear of failure.

Now, a few decades later, I believe there are very few newly appointed leaders who wholly prepare for their new assignment. All need support for what they do.

As a coach and mentor, I realize the top performers are the ones most interested in support. Unfortunately, I see the leaders who most need support are the ones most reluctant to seek help.

To succeed as any general manager, you need to be open to advice, to be coachable. Even with many years of experience, I am still learning; I remember some lessons from forty years ago and others from four weeks ago.

On the following pages, I look at an aspect of CEO leadership, marketing and sales, and try to relate some of the lessons I have learned and valued.

Do I have a career background in sales or marketing? I do not. That is precisely the reason I selected this topic. My early career started as an industrial engineer, followed by assignments in product development. My education and early career background do not provide a pedigree for writing on a topic like marketing and sales.

I doubt any top executives can say they were fully prepared in breadth and depth to manage everyone in the teams who came to report to them. There simply is not enough personal bandwidth to learn everything, especially in a medium or large-size business. Unfamiliar issues and opportunities can challenge leaders.

A lack of education or experience in an area of responsibility does not mean they can delegate responsibility. In the final accounting of events, an owner, a CEO, or a division president is accountable for giving direction to all aspects of their business.

When I was involved in engineering and there was a crisis, we resorted to *meatball engineering*. Said another way, when there is an issue to be resolved and there is little time to weigh the alternatives, a leader must act. Sometimes they must take the most direct solution and run with it. The answer might not be refined, but doing nothing is the lesser alternative.

At many points in my career, I found myself applying meatball practices to marketing and sales.

If you want to keep your organization moving forward, imperfect or incomplete information will, at times, determine decisions. Sometimes, you do not know what you do not know.

This book combines my firsthand experiences as well as my observations of others who dealt with the challenge of directing marketing and sales functions. Most of my leadership direction did not come from an MBA class. Some of what I relate comes from the successes I had in my efforts or saw from the successes of others. Unfortunately, it seems the greatest number and most poignant lessons were the results of bad experiences. I hope you find some wisdom you can use.

1

A PERSON OR A PROCESS?

Many CEO's, founders, and owners I meet express deep regret for someone they hired to manage their marketing or sales efforts. As a CEO coach, typically I hear a story like this, "I hired someone I thought could do the job. It did not work out. They made almost no sales."

The interview was convincing. The candidate told you they worked in marketing and sales since the Stone Age. They professed an array of experiences and success stories. They seemed presentable, likeable, polished, and relaxed.

So why do hiring decisions fail?

Hiring a Marketing and Sales Expert May Not Work

Hiring a professional as the way to grow your sales seems like a plausible choice, especially if you are inexperienced or uncomfortable with marketing or sales.

However, this hiring approach has some risks.

Onboarding. It can take a new person several weeks or months to understand and articulate the value proposition for your business and its intended target audience. There are always things about your company or your industry, which are part of the lore, subtle tribal knowledge.

Misalignment. You might disagree with each other, particularly if you hire someone from your industry. Many companies, especially start-ups, fail because of bad chemistry on the team. There can be personality conflicts and disagreements about selling approaches and priorities. Many conflicts concern pricing and discounts, promotions, and salesperson compensation plans.

False Confidence. You hire them expecting they know what to do simply because you do not know what to do. This should not be taken as a criticism.

We are not perfect in the way we make decisions. We cannot know everything about everything. At the same time, when you hire someone, what evaluation criteria do you use? How do you judge whether they know what to do?

Turnover. You end up with churn in the position, and churn is expensive. After you have hired two or three people into a position, do you think your next hire will be better? You have heard the trite saying, "the definition of insanity is doing the same thing over and over again expecting a different outcome."

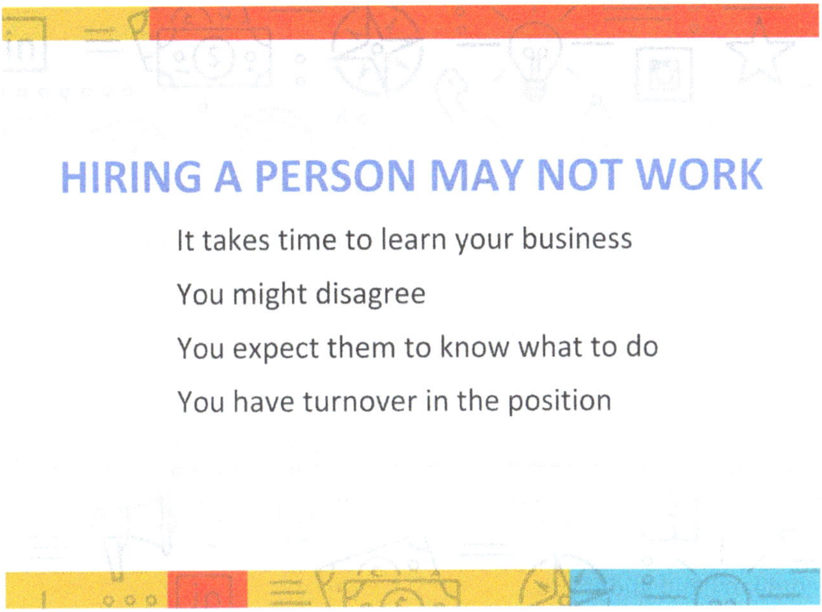

HIRING A PERSON MAY NOT WORK

It takes time to learn your business

You might disagree

You expect them to know what to do

You have turnover in the position

FIGURE 1. Risks you have when you rely on hiring someone to solve an issue.

This reminds me of a baseball story told by Ronald Reagan, former US President and storyteller in his *Our Time Is Now* speech.

> Legendary Baseball Manager Frankie Frisch sent a rookie out to play center field. The rookie promptly dropped the first fly ball hit to him. On the next play, he let a grounder go between his feet and then threw the ball to the wrong base.
>
> Frankie stormed out of the dugout, took his glove away from him, and said, "I'll show you how to play this position." The next batter slammed a line drive over second base.
>
> Frankie came in on it, missed it completely, fell when he tried to chase it, threw down his glove, and yelled at the rookie, "you've got center field so screwed up nobody can play it."[1]

Marketing and Sales is a Business Process

When I coach business leaders about marketing and sales, I encourage them to see it as a process rather than as a person. When you look at it as a process then map the steps and measure results, you end up with a vastly different outcome.

To map the marketing and sales process, the first step I coach is to name and communicate the target customer segment(s) you wish to serve.

Next, the best practice is to align your website and your personal online profiles, so they all say the same thing. Consistency is important as potential customers will go online in advance of any meeting with you to explore and learn what might be told about your company and about you.

Once you do this preliminary work, you can design the way you intend to get leads. You might use social media campaigns, online advertising, blog posts, or email. You might encourage referrals or do cold calling.

Be Willing to Be Flexible

Whatever you do, at first consider your approach to be an assumption and prove to yourself it will work. If not, pivot on your plans and go a different direction until you are satisfied with the results you are getting.

Once you have proven the process for getting leads, what is your method for following up? Do you make sales calls? Do you generate quotes? Do you make presentations? Do you track metrics for these activities?

After you have set up a complete process for developing leads and closing sales, then you can plug people into the process and give them direction. You have a better plan for growth.

Hire a Person Who Fits Your Process

If you have a good understanding of the process you want, you are in a much better position to hire the right people. You can focus your hiring criteria on experience, accomplishments, and personality. You will make better hiring decisions.

The right person for the job is essential. You are the one who must select the right candidate, and you are the one who must give them direction.

You are also the one who must dismiss someone for inferior performance. Retention decisions solely based on contributions to revenue growth contributed to an individual position ignore other factors. Focusing on process decisions for hiring, retention, and firing may improve outcomes.

When revenue growth does not meet your expectations, should you fire the vice president of marketing or the vice president of sales? Both? What if stagnant growth has nothing to do with their performance? Has a competitor appeared or acted? Do you have quality issues? Do you have delivery issues? Is your target customer segment not growing?

Noted statistician W. Edwards Deming[2] said "If you can't describe what you are doing as a process, you don't know what you are doing." When you see marketing and sales as a process, you are better able to judge people on the way they are executing the process. You will make better decisions.

Does Giving Direction Limit Creativity?

According to legend Steve Jobs, "It doesn't make sense to hire smart people and then tell them what to do; we hire smart people, so they can tell us what to do."

I am not buying that quote at face value. The reason Jobs returned to

Apple was to give direction to the company. If the aim was to hire smart people who tell you what to do, the Board of Apple might have acted differently with their hiring decision. Why hire Jobs?

Truly creative people want to know all boundaries and sides to a problem. When you add more constraints, the creative process is more challenging. And to a creative person, there is more satisfaction in solving a challenging problem than solving an easy problem.

It may seem counter-intuitive, but giving direction spurs creativity, freedom from constraints does not. An undefined problem is a problem with no solution.

Jobs did not give his people freedom, he gave them direction. He wanted simple, elegant designs, simple interfaces, fresh styling, and many more attributes. These did not come from freedom.

It took smart people to do what Jobs wanted. Likewise, your job as a CEO is to supply the boundaries and constraints to your people.

DISCUSSION QUESTIONS

1. Is your current sales leader someone you hired to create your process?
2. Is your thinking aligned with your sales leader?
3. Have you had turnover in the position?
4. What direction have you given regarding marketing and sales?

TO PLAY THE GAME, KEEP SCORE

Y ou have a new website. Your social media efforts have expanded. You have an updated personal profile on LinkedIn that complements your business website profile. You have done everything you need to do to increase leads to your business. Does this mean you are ready to take the next step?

Are You Ready to Play the Game?

Do you measure your lead generation success? Is there a process in your business to record and track leads? Do you manage your process from the facts or use gut-feel? In the last chapter, I emphasized the importance of seeing your marketing and sales efforts as a process and not as a person.

If you believe marketing and sales is a business process, it logically follows you need to oversee your process carefully. Simply executing is not enough. You want to be sure that your process is working the way you intended.

Here are some suggestions for managing the lead-generation part of your marketing and sales process.

Your Ideal Customer

To generate leads, everyone on your team needs to understand and agree on the description of the ideal customer for each target segment you serve. You will be more articulate if you can be granular and precise about the demographic description of the decision-makers in your target market segment.

When you are crafting the demographics of your ideal customer segment, it is useful to describe it by mirroring the way a Facebook or LinkedIn ad campaign would describe the same customer group. Use the same filters such as keywords, current or past titles, years of experience, company size, interests, income levels, and location.

If you want to add another level of sophistication to your demographic descriptions, break your initial assumptions into groups. For example, if you believe your target market segment to be companies with eleven to two hundred employees, you might consider creating one group from eleven to fifty, and another from fifty-one to two hundred. As your marketing and sales efforts begin to validate, comparing results from each group could be insightful.

For those who sell Business-to-Business, "Companies who ..." are not the customers. Rather, it is the individuals inside a company with the duty, responsibility, and authority to make a purchase who are the customers.

How can you begin any online search, develop keywords for your website or blog, create an email campaign, or manage a social media campaign if you cannot describe the people you are trying to reach?

What is a Target Market Segment?

For purposes of discussion, a market segment is a group of customers whose purchasing habits are remarkably similar. Usually, customers in a market segment are similar in size and scale. In a B2B customer segment, customers are served in a similar fashion. They may typically be family-owned, partnerships, enterprise businesses, franchises, or solo entrepreneurs. It would be unlikely for a market segment to have all these profiles.

Identifiable customer segments typically make purchases of the same order of magnitude. The decision makers may hold similar positions in the company. They buy the same products or services. The same or similar competitors exist in every sales situation. Segmenting customers is crucial because they interact with you in a similar fashion, and for efficiency you can create one value proposition which applies to all within their segment.

If you find your customer list contains customers who do not act similarly, then you should sort the list into groups of customers that are alike. Chances are you are serving more than one segment. You may need a different value proposition, and you may have different competitors to consider.

Common Segmenting Mistakes

I have encountered several different mistakes that leaders make when discussing their target markets. Here are a few.

Target Uncertainty is a prevalent problem in the start-up community and for many floundering businesses. These businesses are enamored with their product or service and have no idea who will buy their solution. Usually, they rationalize that the strength of their concept is so good; it is merely just another task to find customers. They do not create their product in the context of the jobs, pains, and gains which might be relevant to their segment.

One unintended consequence for this behavior is that they do not know who the competition is when they finally approach a customer. Furthermore, they do not know if their product or service is important to their target customer segment and could waste money and resources building something nobody wants.

Overstatement is an error suggesting a target market that is huge in their pitch deck. They believe that the crucial part of diligence for venture capital funding is to ascertain the size of the potential market. It is assumed that venture capital is more accessible if a large and growing market can adopt your product.

For example, a company suggests their software product is suitable for use in the real estate industry, which is an enormous market. As you understand the product further, however, you find out the product is only relevant to property managers ... of commercial buildings ... which are Class A ... manufacturing buildings ... in multi-unit developments.

The precise customer segment which finds value is much smaller than first described in the pitch deck. When a leader overstates their target market size, further questioning usually reveals they have not really put much effort into determining the size of their market potential.

It may seem ironic, but some of the best business models are those that serve narrow vertical markets. Suggesting bigness in your pitch may not serve your best interests. It is better that your estimates of market size completely align with the exact segment you intend to serve.

Looking Backward. It is common for leaders to describe their market by looking at the growth in the last x years, or by describing the size of the market today.

The correct approach is to look forward. What is the size of the market you intend to serve x years from now? Is it a market that is growing, or maturing, or consolidating?

You should think in terms of describing your opportunity going forward, not the possibility that existed five or ten years ago.

"Wannapreneurship." Some leaders believe they know the target market they want to serve and are anxious to build a product, but they do not know what that product should be.

Some approach their markets with trial and error. They build things simply to see if there is interest.

Small Slice of the Pie. Some pitches suggest the company only needs to get a few percent of their market to be a success. They could be an exceptionally large company even with smallish goals.

The problem with this approach is that you are inferring that most of your target segment will not embrace your product. Furthermore, you might be suggesting that there is a better competitive product. It begs the question, "are you playing to win, or do you just want a participation trophy?"

When you have difficulty describing your target market segment, it becomes difficult to validate your value proposition. It also is tough to convince an investor to have faith in your business plan. Investors want to know how they are going to get a return on their investment. If you do not explicitly define who will buy your product or service, an investor cannot be sure you can create the scale and the revenues necessary to get a return.

MANAGING LEADS

Setting a goal communicates expectations

Using a system for filtering makes best use of resources

Counting and tracking leads creates a leading indicator

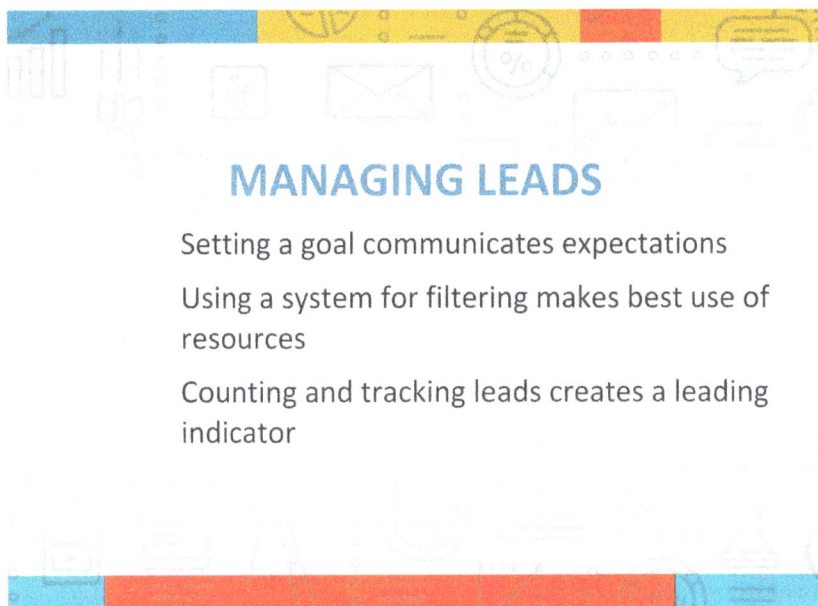

FIGURE 2. Best practices for filtering leads.

Know Your Goal

Once you can be articulate in the way you describe your target market segment, you are ready for the next step.

Are you trying to grow faster than your industry? Are you trying to reach parity with your industry? Do you want to double or triple your business? Executives should set up a goal, even if it seems arbitrary and high. Simply said, if you are going to double your business, you need to double your leads.

You cannot get what you do not ask for. Set a plausible goal that requires some stretch for the organization.

Count Them

I see many businesses in my work, and with most I do not see a system for counting and recording leads. If you do not count leads, you cannot know whether you are getting more or less than last year or last month. Leads can serve as a leading indicator in your business. Understanding trends might be useful for sales forecasts, budgets, resource planning, hiring decisions, and cash flow planning.

Most importantly, a metric must be the best measure of the success of your marketing efforts at the beginning of your process. Do you let the momentum of what you are doing keep you on the same path or do you pivot on your approach?

Twice in my career, my team arbitrarily classified quotes as leads. In one case, 33 percent of quotes became orders. In the other case, 30 percent of quotes became orders. In the short term, the metric was not very precise. However, given a larger sample size over a few months, it was a good leading indicator to use to plan operational resources.

Another notable aspect to this metric was the impact of the size of the quote. Small quotes became orders sooner than bigger quotes. It makes sense as greater expenditures usually need approvals from higher authorities in an organization than are required for smaller quotes. This adds time to the approval process.

Note that a demographic fit was not someone being a lead in our system. In our definition, a lead was someone who was actively searching for our products and services. Do not necessarily take this as good advice. In many business models, a demographic fit is enough.

Some experimentation may be proper to determine the exact definition of a lead in your business.

Filter Them

Be sure that leads are, well, *leads.* Unfortunately, many practitioners declare victory in their efforts by merely counting bodies. Getting more LinkedIn connections, Facebook likes, impressions, or website page-views do not necessarily equate to getting more leads.

The quality of the lead is critical. If the lead is not decision-makers for what you do, or from geography you do not serve, or any reason they do not fit your demographic profile, they are not leads.

Your sales team may have their own way of filtering leads. If they reach out to a customer and sense indifference or lack of urgency on the part of the buyer, they may classify these at once as non-leads. Salespeople will put their efforts into places where they feel they can win.

Sales should not have the final say on what is considered a lead. Some buyers might be a good fit but are not in a place financially, or for some other reason not ready to make a purchase at this time. These customers simply may not yet be ready for the attention of your sales efforts.

You should not pass a lead from marketing to sales unless you have some sign a potential customer has a willingness to make a purchase. The best use of sales resources is to serve customers who are actively engaged in evaluating procurement.

Consider a system for sorting, ranking, and evaluating your leads that includes feedback from sales. If there are attributes that are prevalent among the leads that never result in a transaction, then your lead generation activities should consider this. There is no value added by naming and tracking leads which seldom or never result in a sale. The identification of your ideal customer may be an iterative process.

Lead generation is not the entirety of your marketing and sales efforts. Other steps should follow. Lead generation is but the beginning of your process and success further downstream is not likely if you do not begin with success in increasing leads.

DISCUSSION QUESTIONS

1. Can you describe your ideal customer(s)?
2. What is your goal for growth in revenues?
3. Do you have a system for tracking leads?
4. How many leads do you have today compared to a year ago?

NOT ALL LEADS ARE EQUAL

W hat do you do when you have too many leads? While this is a nice problem to have, it is still a problem. You may have limited resources for follow up and you wish to deploy them effectively.

Chapter 2 discussed the importance of keeping score, measuring the effectiveness of your lead-generation activities. In this chapter, I would like to expand my thoughts about the administration of your sales efforts at the beginning of your process.

Attach Attributes to Your Leads

Some may come from customers too small, others too distant. In addition, some are obviously not a fit for what you do. When you created your social media campaigns, you may have targeted customers on the fringe of your desired profile.

There may also be differences in the enthusiasm a customer shows for what you do. If your product or service is relieving a pain point for a customer, the emotional aspect can sometimes become the most important determinant in the buying decision.

In some companies, the root of discord between the marketing team and the sales team may have more to do with the quality of leads than the quantity of leads. If the sales team finds it is wasting time chasing poor leads (customers not ready to consider a purchase), they may distance from the marketing team and resort to their own methods for generating leads.

If you see this dissonance in your organization, sharpen the focus for your marketing team. The definition of a lead for your business may need added thought and delineation. The sales team should be remain primarily focused on turning leads into revenue.

What you need most is a preliminary way to sort and filter your leads, so you focus on the important ones.

A Way to Assess

In Figure 3 that follows, I illustrate ten leads for a sample business. I presume some industry knowledge for myself and feel comfortable about assessing leads.

For each lead, I have assessed the buying power, which is my way of estimating the long-term value of the potential customer.

Customer	Buying Power	Strategic Fit	Level of Interest
A	$100,000	1	5
B	$200,000	4	8
C	$650,000	9	3
D	$250,000	10	7
E	$400,000	2	9
F	$350,000	2	2
G	$650,000	8	9
H	$600,000	7	6
I	$450,000	3	4
J	$250,000	6	2

FIGURE 3. Estimating fit and interest, an example.

I also added a one to ten rating on my instincts about the strategic fit for the lead. In the last column, I added a one to ten rating for level of interest shown by the potential customer.

In my example, my definition of strategic fit relates to the similarity to your ideal customer. My definition of level of interest would include an assessment of enthusiasm and the immediacy of a potential purchase.

If a lead has already made a purchase of a competitive product, rate their interest extremely low, or consider them not a lead.

Some companies have policies that compel buyers to ask for alternative quotes. You may simply be the alternative in a pre-determined buying decision.

If you expect they may make a purchase at some time in the future and want them on your distribution list for marketing content, you can include them as a lead. Just be sure you are not wasting the time of your sales team.

Unless you are skilled about reading rows and columns of numbers, this tabulation does not tell you much. In the next step, to visualize the difference between leads, I put the same information into a bubble chart.

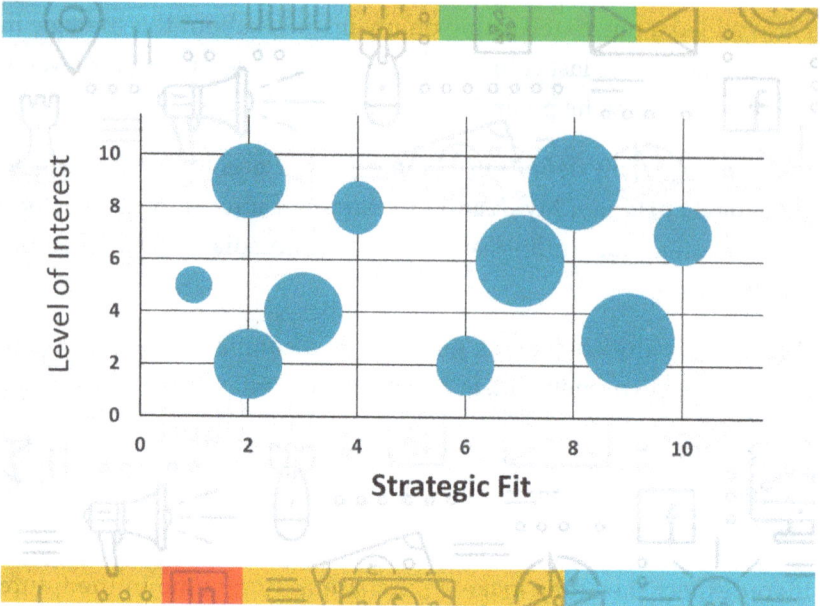

FIGURE 4. Plotting the importance of a lead by fit and interest.

The upper right-hand quadrant has the leads where both strategic fit and level of interest are above average.

The size of the bubble stands for the buying power of the potential customer. In my example case, there are two leads in the upper right-hand quadrant that appear sizable and one that is small.

In the lower right-hand quadrant, note a sizable lead appears where strategic fit is high, but interest is low.

My Interpretation

To manage the leads for this company, focus your first efforts on the two sizable leads in the upper right-hand quadrant where there is a strong fit and high interest. What could you do to increase the interest level of the sizable lead in the lower right-hand quadrant?

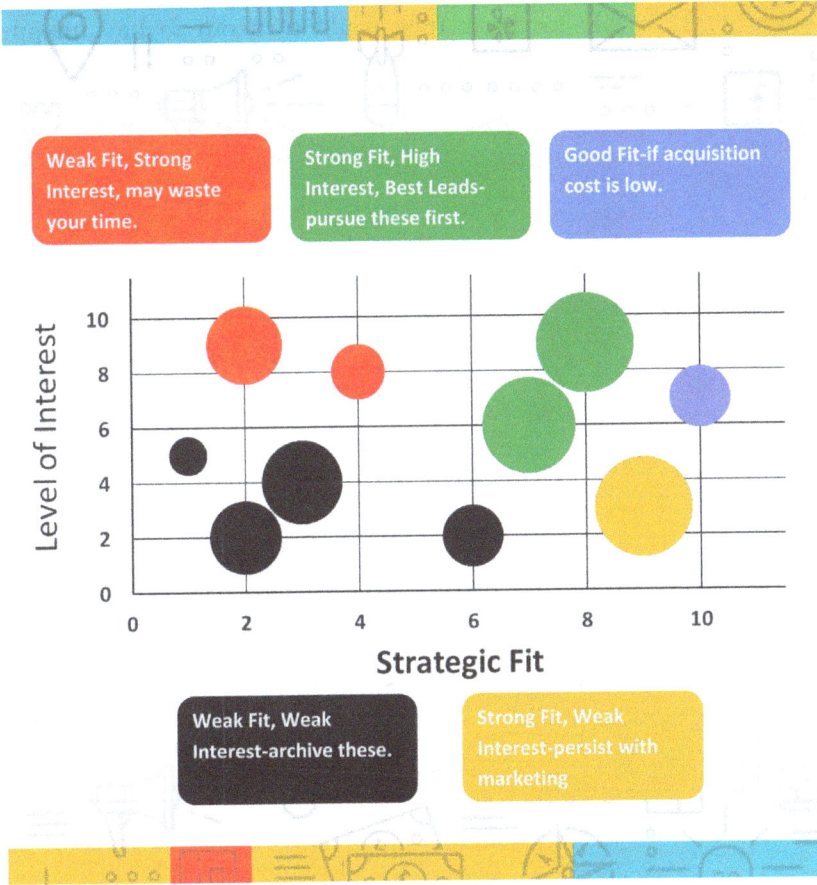

The grid shows "Level of Interest" (y-axis, 0 to 10) plotted against "Strategic Fit" (x-axis, 0 to 10), with the following labels:

- **Weak Fit, Strong Interest, may waste your time.**
- **Strong Fit, High Interest, Best Leads- pursue these first.**
- **Good Fit-if acquisition cost is low.**
- **Weak Fit, Weak Interest-archive these.**
- **Strong Fit, Weak Interest-persist with marketing**

FIGURE 5. Grouping leads.

The cost to acquire a customer might be a consideration with the others. If the cost were high, I would look for more leads as my next step. If the cost to get a customer is low compared to their value, I might consider pursuing the small opportunity in the upper right-hand quadrant.

Obviously, the leads in the lower left-hand quadrant are ones to ignore or archive if there are limited resources.

The leads in the upper left-hand quadrant have risk. These are interested customer leads where the strategic fit is poor. While you might make a sale to these, they could turn out to be unhappy customers in the future. If you do not think your product or service is a fit now, it is unlikely to be a fit later.

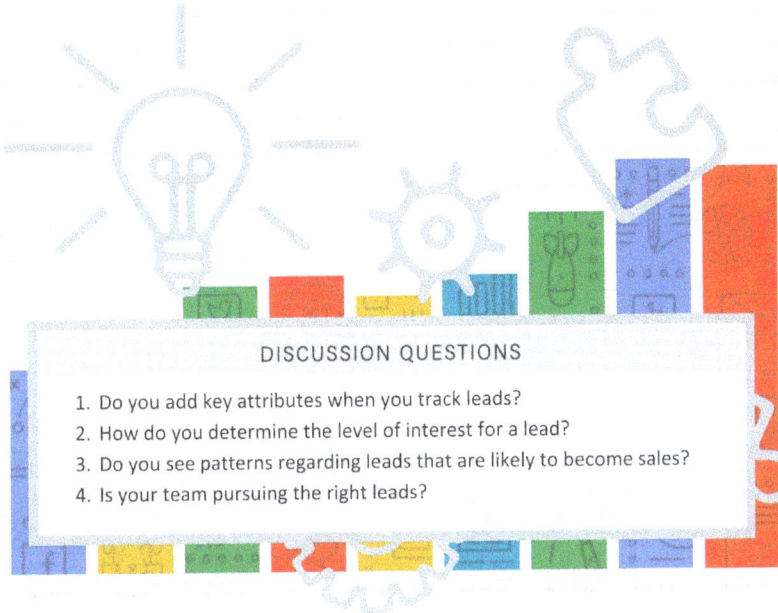

DISCUSSION QUESTIONS

1. Do you add key attributes when you track leads?
2. How do you determine the level of interest for a lead?
3. Do you see patterns regarding leads that are likely to become sales?
4. Is your team pursuing the right leads?

STRONG FIT, WEAK INTEREST

S uppose you identify a lead that is a strong fit for what you do, but when you approach them, they just do not seem interested. In Chapter 3, I noted a lead that was a strong strategic fit and potentially a high value customer but showed a low amount of interest. I suggested you persist with marketing efforts to build interest for this customer.

If yours is a new start-up or a small company, you may have most of your leads fall into this category. The market segment you wish to serve may not know much about you or your company.

What Do You Do Next?

To understand the fix, understand the problem. Likely, you are dealing with people who at first see you as a stranger.

We are all different, but some people may be slower to trust you than other people, your product or service, your competencies, and your company. It may take you time to build familiarity, knowledge, and finally enough trust to make a purchase.

Another possibility is a current budgetary constraint. Another reason for delay might be an issue in their business that needs attention first.

It would be a mistake if you immediately give up your pursuit of leads that seem uninterested but a strong fit. View them as not interested ... yet.

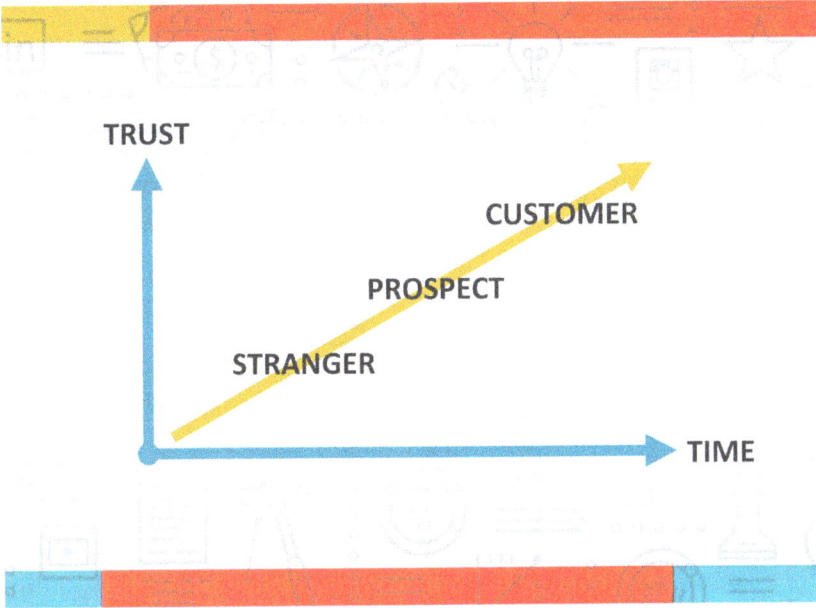

FIGURE 6. Time is required to build the trust necessary to make a purchase.

An Approach to Building Familiarity and Trust

First, establish your own mindset. Your job is to build trust, not to see yourself as a victim of a lack of trust. What you interpret to be rejection may be something else. If your trust-building efforts are insufficient, it is your job to pivot on your tactics. Keep in mind you are managing a process.

Align your personal profile with what you do. Assume that your lead will assess your company and assess you. Many leaders hesitate to put a lot of information online. Some think their title might be too pretentious. Some fear too much bother from too many people. Some fear becoming a target for a nefarious scheme.

My personal feeling is the benefits of being transparent outweighs the risks. If you are the top leader in your organization, people important to you like customers, key partners and potential partners, want to know who the final decision maker is in your organization.

Solicit endorsements from other customers and put them on your website and personal profiles. These days, the first part of anyone's diligence involves online searches. Control what they find.

Be persistent with your digital media efforts such as blogs, postings, newsletters, and all social media campaigns. Many business people foolishly abandon their online marketing efforts before they give them a chance to succeed.

BNI[1], an organization devoted to personal referrals, coaches their members that it typically takes nine to twelve months for others to give you referrals. I believe this is about the same timeframe you should see necessary for online content to be valuable to you.

Promote content that adds value. Helpful hints about your business for example. Establish your **industry knowledge** through repetitive and varied postings.

If you are pursuing high-value customers, **consider doing events** such as a lunch-and-learn. These serve two purposes as they enable customers to see you as a person and an opportunity to prove your industry knowledge.

The Handoff from Marketing to Sales

When a lead does not show interest, I suggest you consider your marketing team to be the *owner* of these leads. Only when the lead demonstrates interest should the opportunity be passed to your sales team.

If you pass the lead and your sales team is subsequently unsuccessful, you not only waste your valuable sales resources, you may also find your salesperson to be dismissive about the opportunity in the future.

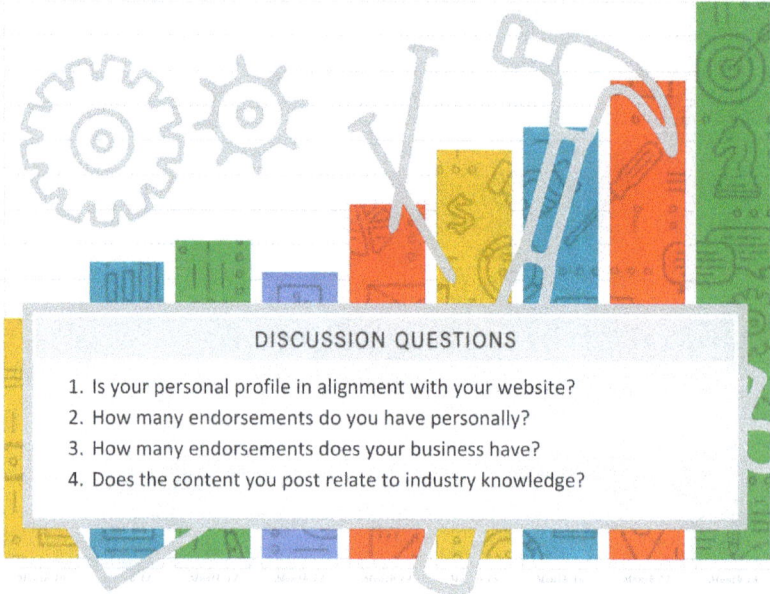

DISCUSSION QUESTIONS

1. Is your personal profile in alignment with your website?
2. How many endorsements do you have personally?
3. How many endorsements does your business have?
4. Does the content you post relate to industry knowledge?

5

BUYING DETERMINANTS

Does the process your target customers use to make purchasing decisions matter? Chapter 4 discussed ways for you to build trust with customers and encouraged you to be patient with the trust-building process.

You can control your behaviors, but your customer is responsible for their behaviors. Their behaviors may have as much to do with closing a sale as yours.

What is the Current Purchasing Decision Process?

If the cost for your product is low, target customers may be able to approve the purchase on their own authority. If the sale involves a high value purchase, the customer may need approvals from their superiors in the organization.

If you are selling a product or service, particularly to an enterprise company, this may be even more complex. In addition to approvals from higher levels of management, you may need approvals from multiple stakeholders from multiple departments who have different, sometimes conflicting, pain points and buying determinants.

FIGURE 7. Involving stakeholders in decisions.

When the selling process is complex, you need a value proposition for every stakeholder. The other choice is to rely on one or a few stakeholders to champion the purchase despite any misgivings by others. I believe this is a way to reduce your success rate.

Likely, your selling process from customer to customer will not vary that much within a customer segment. Most organizations have similar authority levels and you will see a pattern to the way they make purchasing decisions.

This should also influence your marketing and trust-building processes. If you know beforehand the typical stakeholders in your sales process, your marketing processes and social media content should span everyone in the process.

Are We There Yet?

Many purchasing decisions begin when a customer starts their research. This research may take weeks and months. When you ask a customer about the timing for their purchase and they answer, "I don't know," you should not assume they are not interested.

They might be completely open and honest since they do not know when they will be ready for a purchase. They may be unsure about the specifications for their purchase or assessing the possibilities they might have.

When I was specifying automated equipment for manufacturing, I made several trips to Japan and Germany, as well as attending trade shows, just to stay current on the capabilities of the latest factory machinery. When I reflect on this experience, I cannot remember a time when I specified equipment without first understanding the current state of the art.

I may have been uncertain about my specifications and timing, but I was decisive about my intentions to make a purchase.

Some purchasing projects do not have hard deadlines for completion. On the other hand, your creative new product could also spur a buyer into action. If they have been living with a pain point for some time and see no solution, your product or service might be the reason for them to act.

Does Your Process Mirror Their Process?

As you are considering the steps in your marketing and sales process, you might find value in mapping the purchasing processes of your target customer segment. Does the process for the way you create your marketing content and outline your sales efforts mirror your target customers' processes for making a buying decision?

The organization I know that has the most complex, rigid way to make purchases is the US Government. When you are a government contractor, you must be detail-oriented to do business.

In the private sector, there may be less documentation about the process, but that does not mean there is not a process. With the government, the requirements are onerous, but at least you know the steps. In the private sector, you need to do your homework.

A Purchasing Process Case Study

One success story for me involved the US General Services Administration (GSA), the agency which manages most of the purchases for the United States federal government. In the late 1970s, there was a scandal involving the purchase of office furniture by the US government that resulted in sixty-nine guilty pleas or convictions. Subsequent to a Senate Government Affairs subcommittee hearing, all purchases were suspended[1].

To restart their purchases, the management at the General Services Administration changed their purchasing process and created a team to enable the purchase of commercial items.

In 1982, the General Services Administration issued their first commercial item description for vertical filing cabinets. This document described the salient features of the product and the testing requirements necessary to qualify the product. Inspectors from the General Services Administration witnessed the testing.

With respect to my career, I was a recently named product engineering manager. The General Services Administration issued a solicitation and the commercial item description made its way to me. This was not only new to the General Services Administration but also to my company; we had never done business with the US Government.

The solicitation was for more than 32,000 filing cabinets. Success with this project would be spectacular as we were in the depths of a recession where our factories were working thirty-two-hour weeks and management was enduring 10 percent pay cuts.

It was a practice in a General Services Administration solicitation to request quotes for supply in zones; the East, Middle, and Western States, and to ask for pricing for each item in each zone.

We bid on the solicitation. When the winners were announced we found out we won *every* item in *every* zone.

Then, much to our surprise, we found out there was an innocuous line in the contract that allowed General Services Administration to increase their purchases by 50 percent.

They did, on the *second day* of the contract. We had orders for more than 49,000 filing cabinets. Our factories went from undertime to overtime. For us, the recession was over.

The first product was an enormous success for the General Services Administration. Our pricing was 20 percent better than their purchases from three years earlier.

The General Services Administration then followed with a similar process for other products. With each solicitation, there was an opportunity to comment on the specifications. I traveled to Washington, DC and met with the specification writers inside the agency.

This was enlightening. They had no budget for travel and could not attend any industry trade shows or visit manufacturers. They relied solely on comments from people like me.

I also saw a pattern in the way they wrote the commercial item description.

This was the early days of the personal computer and we began to market a line of computer furniture.

I knew the specification writers in DC had no knowledge about this category. I drafted a commercial item description myself. I used the General Services Administration's methodology, then packaged it with a cover letter which said, "If you would ever be interested to write a commercial item description for this, here is my suggestion."

I put this in the mail, then got busy and forgot about it. The truth be told, I did not even tell anyone about my letter; I did it to see if it could be impactful.

About six months later, we received a solicitation for computer furniture. The commercial item description was *verbatim* my submission from six months earlier. You can be sure the specification I wrote excluded most of our competition.

I do not know for sure, but I would guess we sold more than $30 million of that product line to the General Services Administration.

I could not have succeeded with this effort had I not been deeply involved inside the workings of the customer's purchasing process. I knew the people involved. I had not misled them on any previous comments.

I believe many managers and salespeople miss the underlying reasons for motivation for people in large bureaucratic companies or agencies.

In some cases, the people who represent your customer are looking for a promotion. If you can make them a success, it is good for their career. In other cases, people might do business with you because they trust you will not do anything to get them into trouble.

Either way, listening to the needs of the people who manage the purchasing process can put you in an advantageous position for the sale.

Another Way to Rethink Complex Selling Processes

Many start-ups are finding success by creating business models based on recurring revenues rather than large transactions.

You have seen the practice. All new software applications charge by the month with the software hosted on a server in the cloud. WeWork[2] is selling office space and services by the month. Auto companies are experimenting with recurring revenue models that combine purchases, vehicle maintenance, and insurance into one subscription payment.

You can reduce the complexity of your selling process if you can reduce the authority level needed to make a purchasing decision.

This also influences whom you consider a lead. If you are a B2B business and have a high transaction cost, you may need to target vice presidents or other C-level officers. If the cost can be lower, managers and directors can be decision makers. If you are a B2C business, the income levels you target can be lower.

By reducing the cash outlay, you expand the universe of potential leads.

This can also be a higher margin way for you to market your products. Since the out-of-pocket costs are lower, you can create more revenue for yourself than you realized from a one-time transaction. Price resistance is lower for lower-cost products and services.

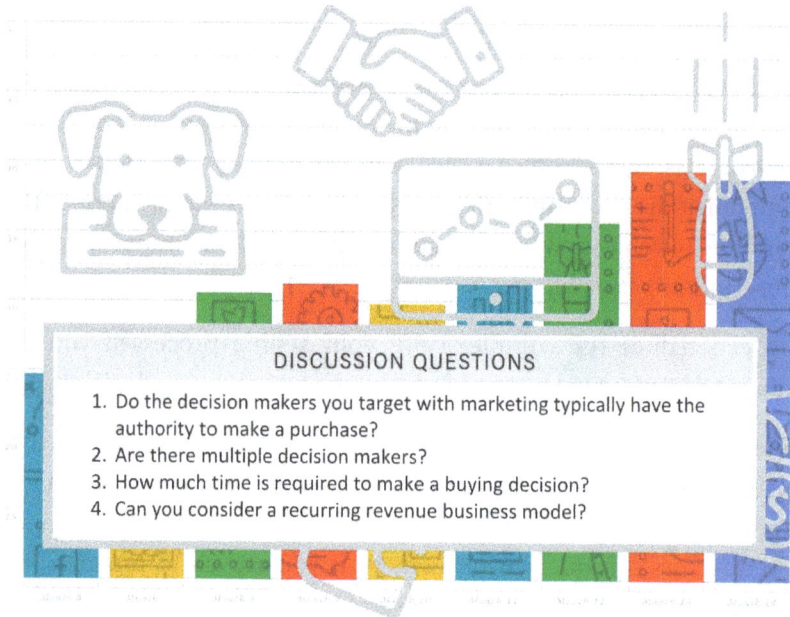

DISCUSSION QUESTIONS

1. Do the decision makers you target with marketing typically have the authority to make a purchase?
2. Are there multiple decision makers?
3. How much time is required to make a buying decision?
4. Can you consider a recurring revenue business model?

6

IMPORTANT METRICS

Whendots is your customer acquisition process considered a success? Chapter 5 discussed the importance of understanding the purchasing decision process typically used by your target customer segment. In lean thinking terms, it is important not to waste time or resources pursuing the wrong decision makers with misaligned tactics.

Can You Improve the Customer Acquisition Process?

Can you reduce the cost? Are there ways to influence the process so it can be more effective?

If you believe there are ways to improve all processes, your answer is yes. When you see business as a series of processes, you can reflect on the steps in the process and look for improvements or ways to cut steps.

To understand improvement, we need to measure the effectiveness of the process. In this chapter, I would like to discuss two important metrics for customer acquisition. Combined, these are also known as the unit economics of your business model. For start-ups that seek venture funding, these are the most important metrics to track.

Two Metrics: Lifetime Value of a Customer and Cost to Acquire a Customer

The lifetime value of a customer (LTV) is the amount of gross margin you receive during the time you retain the customer. To calculate LTV in a recurring revenue business model, multiply the gross margin percent for the products or services you sell, times the average monthly revenue per customer, then divide by the monthly churn (customers lost) percentage.

As a formula:

LTV = Gross Margin % x Average Monthly Revenue per Customer x (1 / Monthly Churn %)

For example, suppose your gross margins are 70 percent, your average monthly revenue per Customer is $200, and your churn rate is 0.5 percent or 0.005.

The formula would look like this:

LTV = .70 x $200 x (1 / .005) = $28,000

While all the numbers in the formula matter, note the importance of the churn rate. In the example above, suppose the churn rate is 2 percent rather than 0.5 percent.

The formula would be:

LTV = .70 x $200 x (1 / .02) = $7,000

As you can see, the value of a customer is considerably different if you have a high churn rate.

If you do not have enough data to calculate a churn rate, what should you use as an estimate? Most advisors will tell you that a 0.5 percent per month (or 0.005) is a good beginning benchmark if you have no better information.

The cost to acquire a customer (CAC) should include all marketing and selling expenses for a month divided by the number of new customers won for the month. The costs should include obvious expenditures and salaries plus benefits. Do not forget costs such as showrooms, collateral materials, mock-ups, and quoting expenses.

As a formula:

CAC = Marketing and Sales Costs / New Customers Won

For example, suppose your Marketing and Sales costs for the month are $30,000 and you won five new customers.

The formula would look like this:

CAC = $30,000 / 5 = $6,000

When Do LTV and CAC Matter?

When your business is an early stage start-up, these metrics do not matter. You will find these difficult to calculate. You do not yet know:

1) the average monthly revenue your customers spend,

2) your margin,

3) your churn, or

4) the cost of acquiring and keeping a customer.

As a start-up, if you have not done this calculation, do not spend a lot of time trying to be precise.

When you first start your business, it is more important to get customers at almost any cost than to worry about the cost of getting them. While you must get customers at almost any cost to make a start-up succeed, you are working towards a sustainable business model that can scale and ultimately creates profits that can repay your investors.

Unit Economics

As your business matures past the start-up stage, unit economics becomes important. The ratio between the lifetime value of a customer and the cost of customer acquisition (LTV:CAC) should be at least 3:1. In other words, each customer should contribute three times more value than the cost to acquire and retain them.

If your LTV:CAC ratio is greater than 3:1, you have a business model that can be scaled if you spend more on acquiring customers.

If we continue with the example from above where the LTV = $28,000 and CAC = $6,000 the ratio calculation would look like this:

LTV:CAC = $28,000:$6,000 = 4.7:1

This is an acceptable ratio.

However, if the LTV = $7,000 in the situation where there was a higher churn rate, the ratio calculation would look like this:

LTV:CAC = $7,000:$6,000 = 1.2:1

This is not an acceptable ratio.

The important mindset for a start-up is to experiment your way to the 3:1 ratio. Do not accept your calculations as an unchangeable relationship.

In a more mature business, if you aggregate expenses properly in your chart of accounts, you can easily track these metrics. For some readers this may be obvious, but I mention it as I have seen many financial statements that never bother to calculate the necessary subtotals.

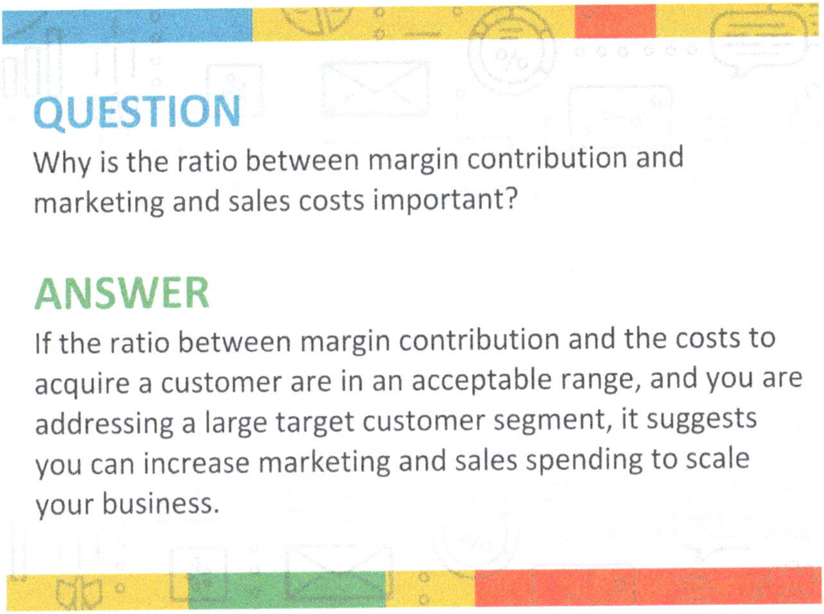

QUESTION

Why is the ratio between margin contribution and marketing and sales costs important?

ANSWER

If the ratio between margin contribution and the costs to acquire a customer are in an acceptable range, and you are addressing a large target customer segment, it suggests you can increase marketing and sales spending to scale your business.

FIGURE 8. *Why is the ratio between margin contribution and marketing and sales costs important?*

Business leaders must direct their accountants to create the proper categories in the chart of accounts. Without direction, most accountants will place salaries for all employees into a single account, not focusing on the need for operational measurements and controls.

When Your LTV:CAC Ratio is Too Low

If you have put the metrics in place and are satisfied with your methodology for measurement, what do you do if your ratio is less than 3:1? Does this mean you have a failed business model?

The first consideration should be to consider other aspects of your financial model.

I served in a business where our margins were about 70 percent. This was unusually high, compared to other businesses I knew, but the margin was sustainable and uniform across everything we sold.

Our LTV:CAC ratio was just under 3.5:1. In practice, we saw the reported metric as an opportunity. We devoted considerable management time and energy to improvement projects. Since there is both a numerator and a denominator in this ratio, your improvement projects could focus on one or the other.

In the situation I described above, we chose to first focus on the numerator, the LTV. We created agreements with others to market their products using our infrastructure. Our existing customers bought more things from us. The result was an increase in LTV with no change in CAC. Our efforts to reduce our CAC were more modest. We reviewed our expenses and selectively reduced some of our spending.

I am also aware of another case, where the owner of a business was concerned about the LTV:CAC ratio. Here, the business realized margins over 60 percent. Relatively speaking, this too is on the high side.

This owner devoted efforts to reduce the CAC. They implemented reductions in salesperson commissions to bring their ratio up, not bothering to fully weigh all the consequences.

I would not advise this. The market determines compensation for salespeople, not an internal metric calculation. The risk is self-inflicted turnover in the sales team. And, as you might expect, the best people, the most marketable people, were the first to leave. The consequent result was an increase in CAC, not a decrease.

If you focus on the numerator in your deliberations, I believe you will have better results. Are you wasting resources pursuing customers who are too small? Are there products or services that can be added?

There are acceptable ways to reduce CAC. If you employ a sales team, consider ways to make the salespeople more productive. Do you have salespeople doing tasks that can be done by your marketing, operations or accounting teams? Can you enable your team to pursue more opportunities?

DISCUSSION QUESTIONS

1. What is your cost to acquire a customer (CAC)?
2. What is the lifetime value of a customer (LTV)?
3. What is your LTV to CAC ratio?
4. What could you do to reduce the cost to acquire a customer or to add to the lifetime value of a customer?

7

WHEN GROWTH IS STAGNANT

S uppose you have been in business for a while, but your revenues are not increasing. Worse, your revenues are declining. Chapter 6 discussed metrics for measuring the success of your process.

This chapter will address a different situation; slow growth, stagnation, decline, or inconsistency in your revenue streams. How should you examine your process?

Fix the Root Cause

If your business is mature and your revenues are stagnant or declining, what is the root cause if you see customer acquisition as a process?

My favorite way to get to root cause issues comes from lean thinking. In lean thinking, the approach is to ask the *5 Why's*.

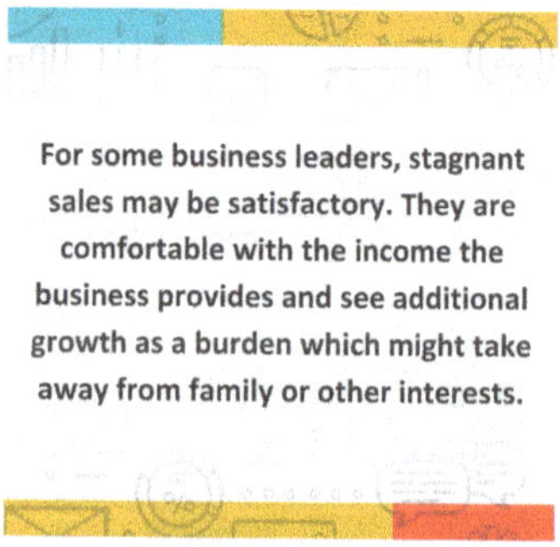

For some business leaders, stagnant sales may be satisfactory. They are comfortable with the income the business provides and see additional growth as a burden which might take away from family or other interests.

FIGURE 9. Stagnant can be a choice.

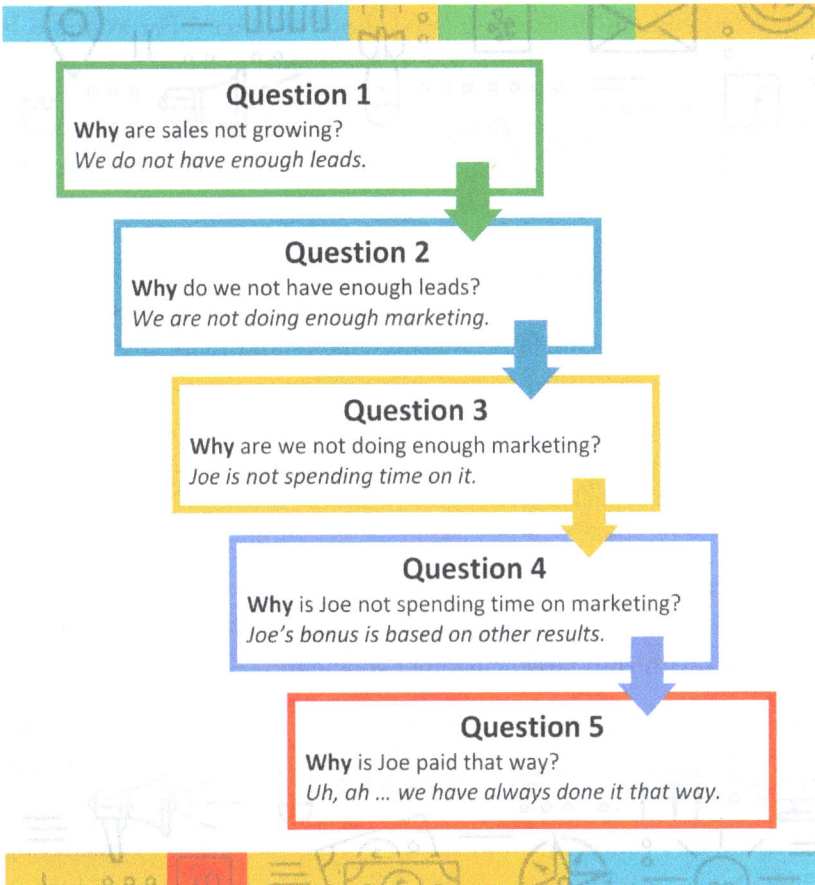

Question 1
Why are sales not growing?
We do not have enough leads.

Question 2
Why do we not have enough leads?
We are not doing enough marketing.

Question 3
Why are we not doing enough marketing?
Joe is not spending time on it.

Question 4
Why is Joe not spending time on marketing?
Joe's bonus is based on other results.

Question 5
Why is Joe paid that way?
Uh, ah … we have always done it that way.

FIGURE 10. Example of a five why approach.

Typical Root Causes

If your revenue growth is stagnant, I encourage you to question yourself and others in the business until you find your root cause(s). It is better to act than to blindly accept your situation.

Are there patterns that repeat? Here are some possibilities; I have seen all of these.

Your customer acquisition process is valid, but you have not made the decision to spend more on customer acquisition. Have you budgeted enough? Is there an issue about resources? For example, is hiring salespeople or spending on social media an issue?

A corollary: you are not confident your acquisition process is valid. Do you need to act? When something is going wrong, it can be stressful. Some people react by doing nothing. They are unwilling to face the issue.

I worked with a business where the sales process was validated, the cost of customer acquisition was acceptable and there was plenty of untapped potential customers. I suggested to the CEO an increase in the size of the sales team.

He had a tough time thinking this solution was prudent. He reacted as though this suggestion was too simple.

Your acquisition process was previously valid, but something has changed. Is there a competitor doing something which changes the dynamics with your target customer segment?

You have organizational misalignment. If there are people in high places in your organization who are not buying in to the direction of the company, you may be sending mixed messages to your target companies. I can assure you target customers who are considering doing business with you are doing diligence. You do not want them to get the impression your company internally disagrees on strategy and tactics.

You suffer from inarticulate communication. There may be good reasons target customers should do business with you, but the way you say it, the frequency with which you say it, and the emphasis you put on key points does not do justice to the benefits of doing business with you.

A Case Study

I recently compiled and reviewed three years' financials for a business marketed for sale. The profitability of the business was steady for the previous three years. You could get the impression this was an established, solid enterprise if you looked only at the cash flow.

However, if you studied the details of the financial statements, a different picture emerged. You could see from the statements from three years ago, a business that was growing about 25 percent over the previous year. The payroll was larger, there were adequate staff, and reasonable amounts spent on marketing.

In the following year, the owner reduced payroll and reduced marketing expenses. The company made the same profits but there was no growth.

In the third year, the payroll was further cut, and marketing reduced to zero. Profits were still the same, but the business now looked more like a turnaround situation.

I could not value the business in the third year, as I would have in the first year.

Sadly, this is not an isolated example. Some advisers coach their clients to cut expenses when preparing a business for sale. They decide marketing expenses are a luxury expense to eliminate.

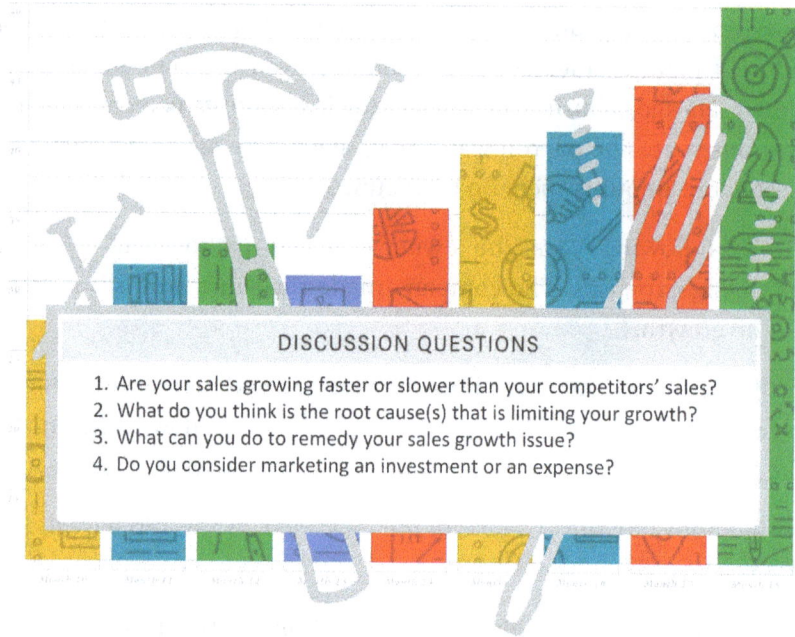

DISCUSSION QUESTIONS

1. Are your sales growing faster or slower than your competitors' sales?
2. What do you think is the root cause(s) that is limiting your growth?
3. What can you do to remedy your sales growth issue?
4. Do you consider marketing an investment or an expense?

8

A COST YOU CAN INFLUENCE

A re costs of customer acquisition controllable? Chapters 6 and 7 discussed the cost to acquire a customer. Should you consider this a fixed cost? Can you reduce this cost?

If you understand the importance of the ratio between the value of a customer and the cost to acquire a customer, then you realize that if you could reduce the cost of acquisition, you could grow your business by approaching smaller (i.e. lower value) target customers because you can maintain a reasonable ratio of value to cost.

Three factors are underlying drivers to your customer acquisition cost. These drivers interact and build upon each other. These are drivers you can influence, direct, and control in your business.

Add to your Value Proposition

Many businesses have a value proposition but struggle with the expression of their value proposition.

In brief, your value proposition is what you do for your customer compared to the next best alternative. For most businesses, the alternative is a competitor. For a few, the value proposition is something which compares to a manual process, automation versus labor for example.

Another way of understanding a value proposition is to explore how life changes for your customer by doing business with you compared to what they were doing before. What is the difference you make? Did they have a burdensome pain point before? Do they have it when they do business with you?

The strongest value propositions are those that eliminate a pain point, remove a hassle, or stop an aggravation for your target customer.

Value propositions can also be emotional. They can make your target customer feel good about doing business with you. Products or services that serve a social good or build community, for example, have value.

To lower customer acquisition cost, you can look for ways to add more to your value proposition. What does your target customer do just before or just after they use your product or service? Whom else do they need to call? How easy is it to do business with you?

Do you do all they need, except one thing? Is there a way you can make your product or service an end-to-end solution?

Uber and Lyft are two examples of end-to-end thinking. Their products eliminate pain points for both drivers and passengers. They eliminate hassles with payment. The vehicle is always moving, not waiting while customers pay or in a line waiting for a fare. Customers know their costs, drivers know their revenues for every trip.

Another useful exercise is to find all the key elements of the competition's value proposition. Is there anything they do which you could add to your business model to obviate an advantage they have?

REPUTATION

What others say about you

Published Endorsements

Demonstrated skills, blogs, videos, photos

PROCESS

Repetition

Preparation

Trained Salespeople

VALUE PROPOSITION

Real, not contrived

Meaningful, important to your target segment

Pain reliever

Stated clearly, concisely

FIGURE 11. Factors that reduce your customer acquisition cost.

If you have a service offered in your business and all your competition does the same, that service is a necessary ante in the game considered by a potential customer, but it is not an element of your value proposition.

Practice Your Process

If you can repeat the process for gaining customers, your skills will improve. Each time you execute the process, you learn something, and you can make subtle but critical changes to the way you deal with every potential customer.

Visualize their experience. If they visit your business, where do they park? How do you greet them? What is the first thing they see? Is the first impression a mess, a dirty lobby, or tired plastic plants?

Figuratively, if not actually, prepare for customer interactions with a scripted approach.

I worked with a business where we picked up customers at the airport with a clean, shiny Mercedes. We dropped them at the front of our business. We greeted and ushered them to a conference room with a view where there was a tablet, a pen, and a bottle of water.

People from the business interacted with them the same way for every visit. Everyone involved from the business knew his or her role and his or her deliverable to the process. We had a remarkably high close rate on these customers.

In contrast, I had a friend who once visited a company and the person picking him up in the morning had obviously been drinking!

When everything is scripted, you avoid misalignment in your message. You leave customers with the impression you know what you are doing, you are confident, and ready to serve.

If your target customer is an enterprise employee, the value proposition might be promotion to a better paying position.

What they do not want is a decision to do business with you that backfires on them.

Control Your Reputation

In the world we live in today, you control your reputation by what people read online. When people consider business dealings with you, especially strangers, their searches are likely to bring up postings to places like Yelp[1], Glassdoor[2], and many other places that ask for comments.

If you have satisfied customers, ask them to give you reviews. Most are pleased to help.

Be sure all the online places where a target customer does diligence are in alignment. Your website, company pages on LinkedIn[3], Facebook[4], and others should all say similar things.

Likewise, your personal profiles and those of your employees should all serve to sell your company.

Online presence is not new, but its importance continues to grow. Those who do not use it are typically baby boomers ... and they are rapidly leaving the business world. The next generations gravitate to online tools.

I recently posted a Yelp review for one of my clients. Admittedly, this client is in an industry where you can be almost certain that everyone considering doing business does online diligence. I was astounded that my review generated over 400 views in the first month after posting.

The conclusion I make is you would be prudent to control what potential customers find and give them a lot to find.

Enhance your reputation by actively showing expertise in your business. Blogs are one way to do this. Sharing relevant content from others can build your reputation. Likewise, hosting a lunch-and-learn for a customer is an effective tool.

The Other Choice is ...

If you have a weak value proposition, a chaotic way you handle potential customers and little or bad online reputation, do you think it will be easy to get new customers?

DISCUSSION QUESTIONS

1. Does your statement of your value proposition clearly differentiate your company?
2. Does your value proposition address a target customer pain point?
3. Do you repeat the process for your sales events?
4. What is your online reputation?

9

TEN AUDIENCES WHICH MATTER

Are you speaking just to customers when you discuss your value proposition? Chapter 8 discussed the importance of articulating your value proposition. Many readers will conclude that the intended message, your value proposition statement, is for potential customers to create demand.

This may be your first motivation, and it may be a good reason for clearly telling the story about your business.

I suggest a broader view. Other audiences receive help from articulation by the leadership of the business.

The Audience on the Inside

Begin with the inside of your business. If marketing, sales, and operations teams listen to and see the way you present the company and

Marketing Team
Sales Team-Promise Makers
Operations-Promise Keepers
Target Customer Segments
Competitors
Investors
Suppliers
Potential Employees
Partners
Community

FIGURE 12. The audience for your value proposition.

the problems you solve for customers, they will mimic your behaviors.

This is not exactly a new concept.

Early in my career, I worked for the Maytag Company. At the time, the company invested heavily in national television advertising with ads that featured Ol' Lonely[1]. *Ol' Lonely* was the Maytag Repairman who was bored because he had nothing to do. The point of the campaign was to emphasize the reliability and long life of the product.

Ol' Lonely was a marketing campaign that could have been a Don Draper idea in a script for *Mad Men*. Every quarter there was a management club meeting, complete with Maytag blue cheese, crackers, and alcohol.

Every recent version of the ad was part of the agenda. Everyone in the company knew we had to live up to that reputation in the way we made everyday decisions in our work. It was a story told on national television.

Any business proposal that threatened quality trumped any decision that might save cost or be associated with another motive. Quality was always the top of the pecking order when it came to considering change. Visitors saw the testing labs, the inspection processes, and the engineering effort devoted to keeping the reputation of the company.

Customers and potential customers will always interact with people on the inside of your business. The greater the alignment in messages and behaviors, the more they will build their trust.

Your employees on the inside will appreciate the efforts you put into articulation. In many companies where articulation is unclear, employees, especially salespeople, will develop their own ways to present your story. The result is confusion and even contradictory messages.

The message also has a role in employee retention. When your employees believe you know what you are doing, they will build pride in their company. Everyone likes to be associated with a winner. An articulate value proposition will enhance that image.

The Audience on the Outside

Where do outsiders learn about your value proposition? The most prevalent way in today's business world is by exploring your website.

The public view of your company on the outside is a message that goes to more than just your potential customer segments.

Visitors to your website may also include competitors, investors and lenders, potential employees, suppliers, partners, and others in your community.

For a big part of my career, I was heavily involved in new product development. This may seem counter-intuitive, but I noticed the more a competitor knew about something we were developing, the more likely they were to avoid copying our efforts.

I will admit that the most of our efforts were not exceptionally unique and not patentable (or worth the time, money, and effort). Our product development goals relied on pushing the volume of new products.

What intrigued me was the competitive behavior. Most people who want to be creative try to be different. There is no personal satisfaction for a creative person to be a copycat.

The competition knew our value proposition and wanted no part in confronting us in a battle where our company strengths were in play.

Investors and lenders also do their diligence on your company. I have seen several situations where analytically a company was a workable candidate for investment, but emotionally not a suitable candidate. Sometimes an investor or lender decides based on gut feel. If your value proposition is clear, they will have confidence you know what you are doing.

Potential employees also want to understand your company. They want to know what it is like to work there. Does management give clear direction? Is it obvious what it takes to advance? Will this assignment look good on my resume?

Suppliers and/or potential suppliers also study your company. If they have a new product or service they believe could help your company, would you want to hear their pitch? Stating your value proposition makes it easy for them to find you. If they really have something valuable, you could receive help from being an early adopter.

There may also be potential partners who are looking for you. They see your company as a partner to distribute their product or service and want to create a revenue stream for both of you. They could also see you as a potential acquirer.

You also want a good reputation in your community. Suppose you need agency approvals for something you want to do with your company. If the community sees you as an asset, your chances for success can rise.

Selling Involves Everybody

If your various constituents work for you, your chances are much better than simply relying on your sales team to grow the business. Consensus about your company's strategies and business plan should be a goal of your communications efforts.

When You Betray Your Brand

I feel I need to add a postscript to this chapter. The Maytag story unfortunately has a sad ending. For over four decades, the brand was associated with reliability. I do not have any inside knowledge about what their management was thinking but I can tell you; it became extremely hard to be a customer.

The Energy Policy Act of 1992, which mandated significant reductions in energy use in consumer appliances, had an enormous impact in the appliance industry. This legislation made older designs obsolete.

The leadership at Maytag wanted to be first to market with products that complied. They introduced the Neptune line of washers and dryers. Maytag's laundry machines were the flagship products for the company.

The earlier products used a design platform that first introduced in 1949. Over the years, most of the product changes were cosmetic. The functional way the appliances performed was unchanged. The heart of the product, the mechanical works, came from a factory built during World War II to build military tank tracks.

Therefore, it had been decades since there was a design change of this size.

I knew the culture at Maytag would not introduce a new product unless it was better than the competition. Maytag might take years between launches. The Maytag dishwasher, for example, was better even though Maytag was a latecomer to the market by over a decade.

Until the Neptune launch, I personally owned a Maytag laundry pair for over twenty-five years. I bought them from the service school at Maytag (a lonely-hearts club) where they had been disassembled and reassembled over three hundred times. They lasted another twenty-five years for me.

Confidently, I bought a Neptune washer and dryer, as I thought I knew what to expect. I was wrong.

In a matter of a few years, I had thirteen service calls. One of the last issues I had was a pump failure. The service call cost estimate was more than a new machine.

This was the final straw for me. I decided I knew enough about Maytag's product manufacturing and assembly techniques to find the offending issue.

I did. I found a bobby pin that fell through the soap dispenser and lodged in the impeller in the pump of the washer. However, I had over three hundred components on the floor around me.

I reassembled everything and voila, it all worked again. Nevertheless, I was now over-the-top angry and embarrassed I had ever bragged about the company to anyone. I wrote a letter to the president of the company expressing my embarrassment, especially with a defect that was avoidable.

He never responded because he likely had too many letters. Rather than being a top-rated product, Consumer Reports now had the Maytag Neptune as a bottom rated product. It was no surprise financial results deteriorated. A few years later Whirlpool bought the carcass of the company and now it exists merely as a brand with little equity.

If the brand represented low cost or another attribute, the quality story might not have had the same impact as I might have different expectations. However, the fact that a brand known for high quality delivered low quality was a death knell for me.

Maytag, RIP.

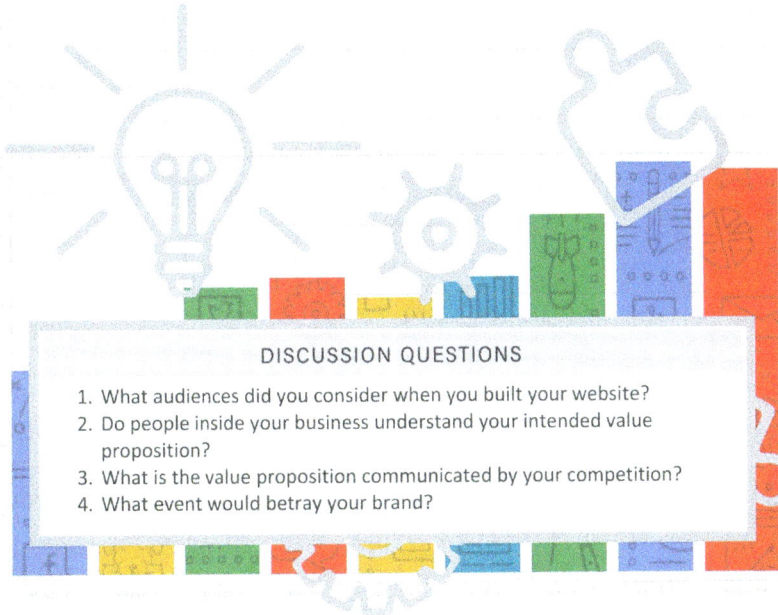

DISCUSSION QUESTIONS

1. What audiences did you consider when you built your website?
2. Do people inside your business understand your intended value proposition?
3. What is the value proposition communicated by your competition?
4. What event would betray your brand?

10

CUSTOMER EXPERIENCE

C ustomer experience defines your brand in an online world. Chapter 9 discussed how your message has both an external and an internal effect valuable to many audiences.

Companies only survive and thrive when they meet the needs and solve the pain points of their customers.

The promise-makers in your organization, marketing and sales, and the promise-keepers in your organization, operations, must be in alignment. Therefore, the messaging you do, on your website and elsewhere, must necessarily radiate in all directions.

There was a time when customers knew your brand primarily from the marketing *promises made*. Today, there are many ways customers perform diligence. They can focus on the actual way you keep the promises you profess. Glassdoor[1], Google[2], and other sites allow people to review your performance. All matter because they represent customer experience as reported by your customers.

What is my definition of customer experience? I see two ways to discuss the topic. There is operational customer experience and strategic customer experience.

Both aspects of customer experience are important. In your role as CEO, delegate the responsibility for operational customer experience improvement to a trusted subordinate so you can devote your time and resources to strategic customer experience improvement.

Strategic customer experience needs change and coordination across many functions in your business, a role for a CEO.

Operational Customer Experience

At one level, I'm sure you recognize customer experience negatives; waiting in line, being put on hold, being misdirected to the wrong person, mistakes in billing, rude customer service, missing web page links, wrong phone numbers, not being able to talk to a real person ... almost too many ways to mention how bad experiences can occur.

One way to create good customer experience is to work on ways to reduce bad customer experience.

I do not wish to take anything away from these efforts to reduce quality issues, as they are important to your business. On the other hand, I view these as operational issues to address, not as strategic customer experience initiatives.

Strategic Customer Experience

In this chapter, I relate two case studies I believe were successful on a strategic level. We devoted hundreds of management hours to making these successful.

CASE STUDY #1

Creating competitive advantage with short lead-times

CASE STUDY #2

Creating competitive advantage with customer-dedicated processes

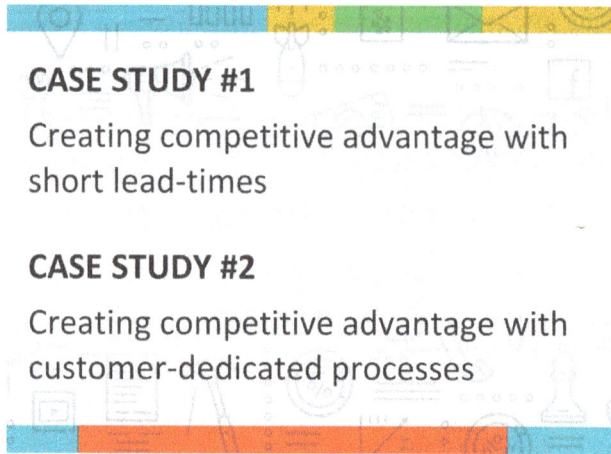

FIGURE 13. Two strategic customer experience case studies.

Case Study 1: Competing with Short Lead-Times

When I served as the president of the BPI Division for HNI Corporation, we had a business that marketed itself primarily to office furniture dealers who sold from retail stores. The company marketed and manufactured low-cost office furniture systems. Typically, retail dealers served small and medium-size businesses in their local communities.

A retail dealer usually had a store with a showroom and a few offices. Salespeople worked on the showroom floor and served customers as they came in the door. Some had warehouses in a second location.

In contrast, a contract dealer had an outside sales team. Rather than wait for customers to come to the retail location, the contract salesperson would find projects and pursue the architect, designer, or facility manager who most influenced the purchasing decision.

The value of the customer versus the cost of a sale meant a contract salesperson did not serve most small businesses.

Small businesses do not always plan everything and might sign a lease for a new space or expansion of their business that involved hiring more people. Faced with a deadline for a move and already having a relationship with a dealer, the small businessperson would usually go to the nearest retail dealership, explain their issue, ask what and how soon could it be done.

This was our critical moment. We wanted the retail dealer to suggest our product line. This was the important focal point of our overall strategy.

The first part of our solution was to offer our product line three separate ways where the dealer could respond quickly without a long lead-time for the products.

Fast. The first way to buy products from us was to order normally where our lead-times from order to shipment were three weeks. Shipping typically took another week, so a dealer could promise four weeks and be able to perform. About 40 percent of our business ordered in this fashion. This was also the way to get the best price from us.

Faster. The second way a dealer could order was to request a five-day lead-time from order to shipment. Including delivery, a dealer could be ready to do an installation in two weeks. We charged more for this, at first about 5 percent. This was also about 40 percent of our business.

This marketing program gave us some operational heartburn. Orders did not flow in a constant manner and there were times where we took Monday off but worked Saturday in the same week.

We decided to raise the price for the five-day lead-time to a 7 percent premium over the normal program to see if we could get business to align more with the three-week delivery.

It did not work as we intended. There was no detectable shift in the way dealers ordered and no complaints. The extra charges went to the bottom line (unlucky, huh). To understand fully, consider that most businesses, ours included, strive to make about 10 percent profit.

With the tweaking of one marketing program, we increased our profits by 20 percent on 40 percent of our business.

Fastest. The third way we set up was to have most of our key products available through a wholesale channel of distribution. Over fifty wholesale locations carried our products. A dealer could buy from the wholesalers who would typically deliver in forty-eight hours or less. The downside was the wholesaler charged about 25 to 30 percent more than what a dealer would pay if they bought directly from us.

This was fair. That was the value added by the wholesaler. This channel of distribution worked very well for us. There were many situations where it was necessary to deliver products in that period.

We spent hundreds of hours changing our manufacturing processes to be just-in-time. We processed development projects to where we could manufacture any product in any color in any order with no set-ups and no cost for one-at-a-time production.

We did not do this with work-in-process inventory. Instead, we cut set-ups. Our work-in-process was so low the accountants counted it only once per year.

We also implemented daily factory scheduling. The earlier method was to schedule everything once per week.

We followed this with more additions to our value proposition.

We created a unique guarantee, *On-Time or On-Us*. What we meant by this was we would pay the freight for the customer if we did not ship on time.

Next, we launched *BPI University*. Dealers could send their operations people to a hands-on class where they could learn best practices in installation.

We examined the specification part of our ordering process and became the first company in our industry in the US to create a library of products for CAD Space Planning, saving a dealer's time in the specification process.

Creating a strategic customer experience is a complete team effort, not just something done by sales, marketing, and customer service departments.

Our brand became associated with short-lead times. I remember situations where we knew we would miss a shipment date because of a product quality issue. We reacted by air freighting the shipment to not violate our promises.

The organization knew the cost for doing this and it did not take long for internal business practices to evolve to the place where we never again had to air freight.

For the dealers, our product line became their single highest-margin offering. In visits with dealers I would assert that fact, challenge them to dispute what I said. Not once did I get an argument.

Last, but not least ... the division grew revenues five-fold.

Case Study 2: Competing on Time to Market

Here, I served as division president for APW Enclosures, a division of APW Worldwide. My division made technical enclosures for OEMs such as IBM, HP, Cymer Laser, Applied Materials, Data General, Sun Microsystems, Qualcomm, Silicon Graphics, and several others. The technical OEMs made their widget; we made the cabinet that housed it. These were typically the size of a refrigerator or larger, high-value, low-volume, with many configurations.

In addition to the box, we installed power supplies, fan trays, cabling and harness, backplanes, and other items that were not the OEM widget. We also had an internal supply chain that could supply injection molded components, electronic assemblies, and machined parts. There was little need for Tier 2 partners.

We coined a self-serving terminology. We boldly referred to ourselves as a Level 5 Supplier to communicate our value proposition. Level 1 competitors made metal parts, Level 2 competitors made assemblies, Level 3 competitors made cabinetry but just the box. Most of our competition operated at Level 3. A few Level 4 competitors did some component integration.

As a Level 5 Supplier, we could do it all. There was no need for another Tier 1 supplier to serve the OEM. I was quite pleased one day when an OEM client used that terminology in a discussion with us. I knew the origins.

Our industry was fragmented; we had many competitors. Before the formation of our company, to distribute around the world, OEMs had to find, qualify, and manage multiple suppliers for the same item in various parts of the globe. The business plan for us was to get suppliers in all key distribution areas where the OEMs manufactured and become the first single-source supplier.

The pain point we found had to do with time to market. In the world of technical products, the first OEM to market usually makes great profits, the second might do ok, but if you were slower to market, you never got enough traction to be a meaningful competitor.

To address this pain point, we needed to show that doing business with us was the most assured way of being first to market.

Our solution was to offer three ways we could serve an OEM. They could make choices about the customer experience they wished to have.

Shared Resources. For OEMs who did a small amount of business with us, typically less than $5 million per year, we placed their business in a shared resource work cell. In this approach to serving them, their orders manufactured using the same equipment and processes as other OEMs.

In this type of manufacturing, the first orders received are the first manufactured. We placed an OEM's order in a queue.

Dedicated Equipment. For OEMs who could give us business from $5 million to $15 million, we would create a work cell dedicated solely to them. Dedicated work cells allowed us to create a just-in-time workflow.

When an OEM would place an order, we could ship it at once. The shipment triggered the work cell to create replacement products. This is a pull system.

This was a much better customer experience. OEMs unfailingly made many shipments at the end of the quarter.

In the shared resource approach, the customer's order triggered the creation of parts and pieces for their final assembly. Sometimes this might take weeks to do depending on the size of the order queue. With dedicated facilities, the pull system was able to replace continuously the final assembly.

Dedicated Equipment, Dedicated Team. The third customer experience served customers who would commit to more than $15 million in annual purchases.

For these customers, we not only supplied dedicated equipment, we added a dedicated staff. Our people became experts in our customers' products.

Most customers wanted this choice.

To make this approach work, we had to be experts at designing and manufacturing cabinetry for technical equipment. The brightest engineers at a technical OEM wanted to be involved in the design, specification, and development of the OEM's widgets. Designing cabinets was not an attractive way to progress in your career at the OEM.

I recall one case where an OEM approached us to get our drawings, as chaos in their own engineering departments resulted in the loss of all their cabinet specifications. Our information became the restore point for re-creating their intellectual property.

Another way we helped the relationship was to have one seat of every major supplier of CAD software. We had our native system but did all the translation behind the scenes. We also had to be good at implementing revisions. Technical OEM's seldom freeze their designs.

To keep our Level 5 status, we also did bolt-on acquisitions to the business for technical or geographic considerations. We bought a facility in Austin, Texas for example. By serving Applied Materials locally in Austin, we were finally able to earn preferred supplier status.

To serve outdoor telecom customers, we bought a company with thick backplane capabilities. As customers included more sophisticated power supplies and other peripheral electronics, we bought a company capable to produce the electronics.

We also had to become experts at costing. I recall a case where we produced a cabinet that sold for about $1,200. Our customer wanted us to buy and install a $15,000 power supply.

We developed a costing algorithm that considered the inventory turns on a third-party item. If the third party could give us weekly deliveries, we could see fifty-two turns and be reasonable with our charges. If the lead-times were longer, our turns would be less, and we would increase the amount of the handling charge for the item. It was a win-win approach.

Our biggest facilities were in Southern California. Because of their location, cost structure and business practices, they became the highest profit factories in the corporation.

We also won the biggest contracts in the industry.

Giving Direction

Both case studies resulted from a strategic plan led from the top. They did not just happen by themselves. Senior management *gave direction* to the efforts.

In both cases, I know there was also strong alignment amongst the senior management team. There was almost no second-guessing about the big picture.

In today's world, there would be other enhancements to the customer experiences. Collaborative project management tools in the cloud would be part of the program. Orders, receipts, billings, quality reports, and other paperwork can use electronic data interchange applications.

If done today, our email marketing and social media content would center on the intended customer experience. We would discuss the value of competing based on lead-times, the simplicity of doing business with us, and the practices our customers should do to take the best advantage of our services.

The biggest difference in the current business environment would be a shift to some form of a subscription pricing model. Increasingly, customers are looking for suppliers who adapt to this method for payment.

All the products and affiliated services would package into a single monthly fee. If you need an office, fast-growing WeWork is the leading example of the way businesses get and use office space in a subscription-based model.

Similarly, people who use technical equipment are buying the services from a subscription supplier like a network-operating center.

If you conceive a way to sell your product or service in a subscription model, you should be executing on a plan to move in that direction. If you do not, it may not be long before a start-up in your industry will build their brand around the strategy.

Continuous Improvement

Do not adopt the mindset you can reach a point where you have the ultimate customer experience.

There is no such thing as a completed plan in the sense you are finished with the design of your process. The better way to think about it is to see it as something that is ever changing to be better. There will be changes in technology that enable you to do different things and adjustments by your competitors.

Make it clear to your organization you are promoting continuous improvement, not the flavor of the month.

DISCUSSION QUESTIONS

1. What are the biggest issues in your operational customer experience?
2. Do you have a plan for customer experience?
3. Does your customer experience plan add to your value proposition?
4. What is your last important customer experience change?

11

FOLLOW THE MONEY

Not all customers behave the same. Chapter 10 focused on customer experience and the importance of removing pain points.

If you believe your customers get value when they buy your product or service and you believe in treating people with dignity and respect, should you also consider supplier experience? Should we view relationships as a two-way concept?

Conventional wisdom teaches *the customer is always right*. Not so.

I've seen behavior from customers which ranges from mildly irritating to completely egregious, bad enough I've literally fired customers.

As a CEO managing your marketing and sales process, inevitably you will face issues which get pushed to your desk. The most angry, most misbehaved, most obstinate, and most relentless customers will be your problem.

Most Frequent Issue: Collections

If your means of doing business is a transactional model rather than subscription-based, you will be faced with the prospect of invoicing and collecting money.

In many industries, suppliers are expected to extend credit terms to their customers. If your terms are payment in thirty days, some customers will pay in thirty-five days. Some will push it further, to forty-five or sixty days or even longer. Some customers will deliberately not pay until your company attempts collection the second or third time.

There are also customers who will create static in the system. "We didn't get the invoice", "Can you send us proof of delivery?" and "Our system is behind," are typical ways customers will deflect their obligation to pay.

In one particular case, we had a customer who was a frequent buyer and did a decent amount of business. But they would chronically delay paying us until we had a thirty day past due bill.

They also wanted to have meetings with management seemingly about every two months. Usually the stated issue was something which turned out to be trivial or not true at all. I believe the real reason for needing attention was to create reasons so they wouldn't have to pay.

Another tactic was to argue for special products, usually minor changes which did little to differentiate from our standard offerings. The customer also wanted special discounts. Another regular approach was to threaten to switch to a competitor for supply.

I was convinced these behaviors were just to ensure we would continue to be a source of working capital for the business.

Finally, one day, this customer started a discussion with one of our best customer service representatives encouraging her to go to work for one of our competitors.

I can only speculate about the thought process for the customer in this situation. Did he think he could do just about anything and we would tolerate his behavior because his business was too valuable to us?

In my mind, he had finally crossed the line. I drove to his business without an appointment, went to his office, confronted him about this latest issue, and told him could place no further orders with us until he was current with his payables to us.

We never did business again.

We retained our customer service representative. The customer switched to a competitor who gave him a much smaller line of credit (there are no secrets between credit managers), no special products, and no special pricing.

He went bankrupt in the 2008 recession.

Should Salespeople Assist in Collections?

Some companies ask their sales teams to become involved in the collection process. This is a mistake.

The person assigned to make collections should be independent of anyone on the marketing and sales team including the CEO of the business.

The first reason for this is salespeople want to sell-sell-sell. They see collection activities as a distraction which takes time away from their selling activities.

The second reason regards the perceived-negative messages which sometimes must be delivered. When non-payment becomes chronic or extended by many days, it is only prudent to suspend sales to these customers. A salesperson whose task it get customers to buy is not very interested to tell customers they can't buy.

Collections, credit line approvals, decisions to suspend purchases, and decisions to halt purchases should be a part of your accounts-receivable processes; not your marketing and sales processes.

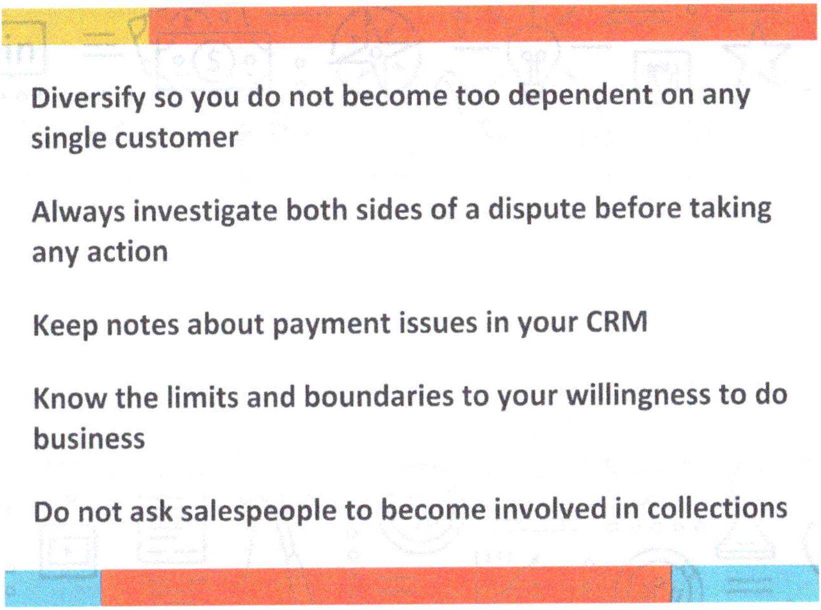

Diversify so you do not become too dependent on any single customer

Always investigate both sides of a dispute before taking any action

Keep notes about payment issues in your CRM

Know the limits and boundaries to your willingness to do business

Do not ask salespeople to become involved in collections

FIGURE 14. *Managing customers and accounts receivable.*

You want to keep your salespeople focused on selling, your sales commission programs should pay for orders invoiced. Some companies calculate commissions based on invoices paid, thus indirectly pulling salespeople back into the collections process.

Salespeople should sell. Your accounting department should determine and approve credit lines and perform collections. To do otherwise invites intramural finger-pointing in conflicts.

When credit line disputes occur, however, it is important to keep your salespeople aware of any issue. It's also embarrassing for a salesperson to be uninformed about one of their customers. It would be a good practice to have your accounts receivable team keep notes in your customer relationship management (CRM) system.

Likely there will be a time when a customer is angry about getting cut off by your collections efforts so they call you to elevate the issue.

One of the lessons I learned from experience is to always promise you will investigate what is going on rather than reaching an immediate decision based solely on the story told by the customer. Maybe I was fortunate to have competent accounts receivable managers but I cannot recall a situation where there wasn't more to learn.

And almost always, our collection efforts were prudent and reasonable.

You will find your customers have a variety of approaches to paying invoices. Your smartest customers will use a three way matching process for paying their bills.

1) The amount they receive must match,

2) the amount they ordered which must match,

3) the amount which is invoiced.

Your operations and invoicing teams must keep accurate records to avoid collections issues.

Fraud

In another case, we had a customer who claimed to have a quality issue and they wanted us to replace their products. This issue was suspect from the beginning.

The product was exclusively for indoor use, partially manufactured from steel. The customer claimed our product had rusted. This seemed very unusual as we had shipped hundreds of thousands of these products and never experienced this complaint.

We slowed our response to reflect on this, but the customer persisted. Unfortunately, for the customer, the next call they made to our customer service representative went to voicemail, which the customer did not notice.

Our voicemail dutifully recorded the conversation as the customer explained to someone in his office how he was "dealing with a stupid b*$#h," and how easy it would be to get free product. I guess people think being a bully in business is a skill.

I must admit I enjoyed returning the call.

Turning Lemons into Lemonade

One of the toughest situations is when you have a customer declare bankruptcy when they owe you money.

We had a case where a customer owed us more than $100,000 and went bankrupt. Fortunately, it was a Chapter 11 Bankruptcy (reorganization).

The day following the notice; I directed our accountants to extend another line of credit, but with a lesser discount on their purchases. The customer was extremely pleased as we were initially the only supplier to approve doing business with them.

During reorganization, you reduce risk as the courts are managing the finances of the business. In six months, we recovered all we had lost in the bankruptcy and kept the customer who was now extremely loyal to us.

Lemons

There was a second similar lesson I regretfully learned which did not have the same positive outcome. Our accountants received a bulk sale notice from a customer that said the customer was intending to sell their business.

By the time we realized and reacted, the business sold in an asset sale. The buyer did not assume the accounts payable obligation and the seller bankrupted their business.

There were not enough assets staying in the original company to pay us and others (a bank or another institution) had senior debt. We got nothing.

Supplier-Managed Inventory

When you extend credit to a customer, the courts consider the customer's obligation to you to be unsecured. Your claims to funds in the bankruptcy are subordinate to secured creditors. Secured creditors are typically the ones who press for legal action.

The only way to circumvent this situation is to create a consignment agreement. In a consignment agreement, you keep ownership of the product until something triggers a change of ownership, typically a sale of the item. If you do this, be sure the items or package are clearly marked and identifiable, so the items do not get lost in a confusing situation.

Many companies have a distaste for consignment agreements due to lack of control. There is a saying "possession is 9/10 of the law." Managers fear something might go wrong if goods are not in their physical control. Theft is a possibility.

I can attest to a situation where consignment was successful. In this case, my company was a customer. We bought pallets of sheet steel wrapped in heavy paper and secured with steel banding. We had a designated spot in our factory for each item we bought. There were different thicknesses and sheet sizes. We painted horizontal red lines on the wall behind the designated storage locations.

If the stack of steel blanks was lower than the red line, it was a signal to the supplier to deliver another stack. If we cut the bands and/or removed the stack, the event was the signal that determined we accepted ownership to the material and triggered invoicing from the supplier.

This was a valuable experience as a customer. The steel wholesaler managed our inventories for us. The unit loads of steel were always the same size. The system worked without counting systems and faith in Enterprise Resource Planning (ERP) software.

In lean thinking, this is a pull system. You replenish inventory only when it is pulled by the next step in the process. Some people call it visual control. Rather than having excess inventory in place and at risk for the rare event just in case something goes wrong, the system trusts reliable triggers.

In another variation of supplier-managed inventory, we created stacks in two separate buildings, one belonging to the supplier (us) and one belonging to the customer. We then installed web cameras focused on both inventories. We could see when the customer consumed our inventory and the customer could see we were prepared and ready to replenish their inventory.

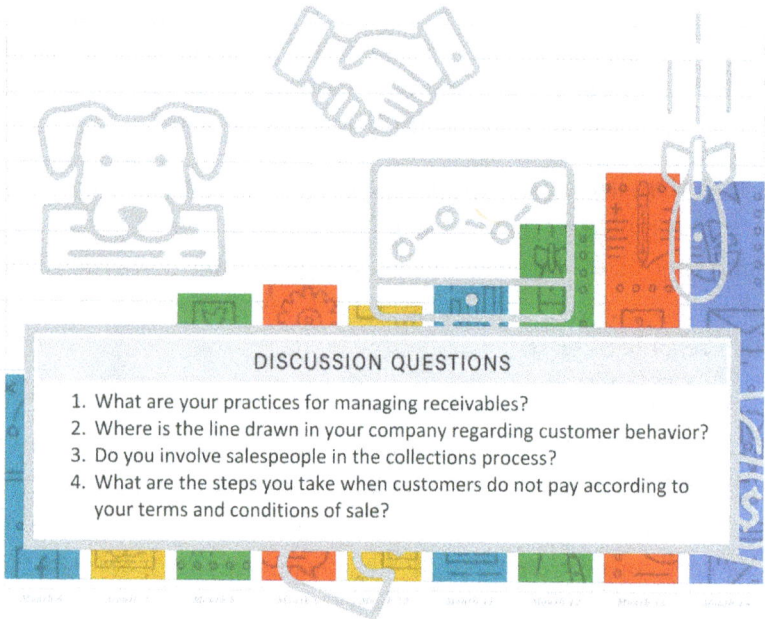

DISCUSSION QUESTIONS

1. What are your practices for managing receivables?
2. Where is the line drawn in your company regarding customer behavior?
3. Do you involve salespeople in the collections process?
4. What are the steps you take when customers do not pay according to your terms and conditions of sale?

12

CHALLENGING YOUR CUSTOMERS

A useful book for expanding your understanding of sales as a process is *The Challenger Sale* by Dixon and Adamson.

The authors' intended audience for *The Challenger Sale* is sales executives and sales managers in enterprise businesses. There is considerable similarity to our perspectives.

The Challenger Sale was published in 2012 and reacts to the chaos from the Great Recession. While those events are fading, relevant and timeless takeaways can still be learned[1].

You can classify Sales Approaches. Based on a study of 6,000 participants, Dixon and Adamson note their researchers were able to find five types of sales reps[2].

A plurality of top performers are Challengers. According to the statistics presented by Dixon and Adamson, 39 percent of the top-performing sales reps in the study came from the Challenger profile[3]. Note the *least* probable way for you to develop a top performing sales representative is to focus on relationship building.

CHALLENGER: understands the customer's business, has a unique perspective

LONE WOLF: follows own instincts, acts self-assured, difficult to control

HARD WORKER: always goes the extra mile, does not give up easily

REACTIVE PROBLEM SOLVER: reliably responds, detail oriented, solves problems

RELATIONSHIP BUILDER: has a good relationship with everyone, generous in giving time

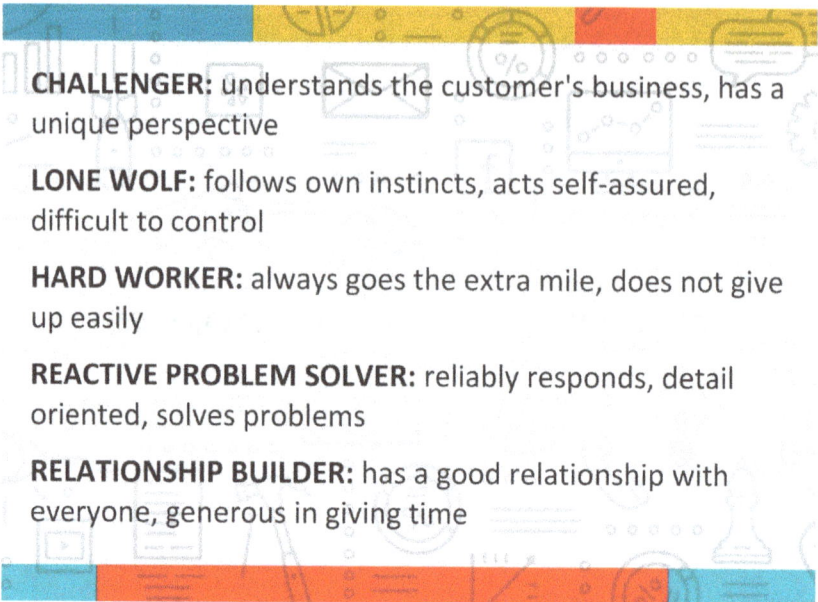

FIGURE 15. Distinct profiles for salespeople. Adapted from Dixon and Adamson.

Perhaps there is also merit to what Dixon and Adamson call the Lone Wolf profile. This is the other profile with a disproportionately higher number of top performers.

The issue with the Lone Wolf profile is that, by definition, this profile is a sales approach which cannot be easily taught, replicated, and scaled.

In small companies, the Lone Wolf might be created by circumstances. The sales team might be small, might be acting without skilled leadership, and might have little or no direction about value propositions or business models. To succeed, salespeople figure it out by themselves.

Why Are Top Performers Valued?

While this varies by company, top performers produce one and a half to four times as much as the average performers. As the complexity of the sale increases, the difference is greater. Dixon and Adamson cite the example of one company with one hundred salespeople where 80 percent of the sales were the result of the efforts of just two people[4].

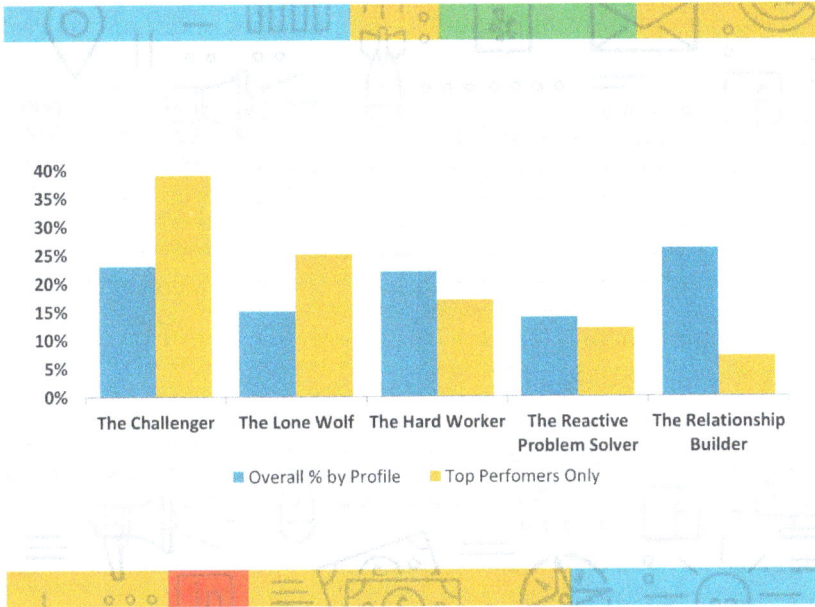

FIGURE 16. Example of the five types by profile and top performers. Adapted form Dixon and Adamson.

Clearly, there is a case to put an effort into finding and developing top performers.

Creating a top-performing sales team might also be a critical element to the success and survival of your company. If you wrestle with keeping the cost of customer acquisition low enough to have a scalable business model, having top-performers on your team can reduce the cost of customer acquisition.

It should also influence the revenue per customer. Top performers should have greater customer retention and the ability to win bigger customers.

Bill's Story

Challengers teach their customers about their own businesses. They bring value to the customer because they can recommend on choices a customer can make and explain the implications of various choices.

Early in my career, I worked in a B2B business and had the opportunity to travel with Bill. If I reflect on the experience, I see Bill as a Challenger. I saw Bill walking into a customer's business and stopping everything with his presence. Every activity paused. *Bill was there* and he was the advisor and mentor to the business. Immediately, I could see Bill was a respected and trusted advisor.

Bill told me about a situation with a customer. He watched his customer for several months and was concerned because it was clear the customer was not making a profit. After some reflection, Bill went into the business one day and told the owner his accountant was an embezzler.

Bill did not have access to the financial statements. He came to his conclusion based on his intuition about the situation.

The owner asked Bill to leave the business and never come back. The accountant was a close friend to the owner and godfather to the owner's children.

Six months later Bill got a letter of apology. While they were angry about the accusations, the owner investigated. They found money in thirty-three different banks.

Was Bill a top performer? Yes, he was salesperson of the year for my company.

The Implications for Your Marketing Efforts

While top performers can come from any of the profiles, what the authors are suggesting is an effort to support challenger selling to increase your odds of creating top performers more than 5 times the effort to support relationship building.

LinkedIn agrees but says it differently. While encouraging their members to, "engage with insight," LinkedIn says, "89 percent of buyers turn away if the professional doesn't have insights or knowledge about their business."[5]

The content in your blogs, emails, and newsletters should primarily teach your customers about their businesses. If you are interacting with your customers, you see patterns that lead to success and see ways to grow not generally seen if all a customer knows is about their own business.

On the other hand, you could see a creative business practice one customer is doing to solve an issue that another customer could also adopt.

Considering the earlier discussion about the importance of customer experience, a content strategy that focuses on teaching can become part of your customer experience.

As I have mentioned before, your content speaks to many different audiences. Content that teaches will be valuable not just to your customers; consider the impact on the new people in your organization.

The Golden Rule for Sales

Early in my career, I served in a role as product engineering manager for a manufacturing company. The responsibility of my organization was to supply the operations and manufacturing engineering organizations designs and specifications. In the world of engineering at the time, you communicated design intent with prints and bills of material.

If a print was silent on an issue, that meant no limitation to what the factory could use. For example, if the print said cold rolled steel but nothing else, a buyer could use any supplier.

At the next level of control, the print would list specific suppliers, whose products were qualified through our quality evaluation processes.

At the highest level of control, when we were convinced that specific features were important, we would specify a specific product from a specific supplier. My organization was sometimes highly influential in the process for supplier choice, particularly when a specification was precise.

As I reflect on this today, the sales representatives who were the most valuable in the deliberations surrounding specifically engineered products were the ones who could show me the best way to incorporate their products. Usually these were trained factory representatives; in other words, Challengers.

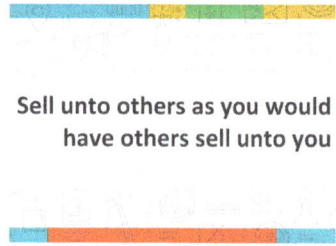

Sell unto others as you would have others sell unto you

FIGURE 17. *The golden rule for sales.*

In contrast, companies represented by independent sales representative organizations were the most frustrating. They could seldom recommend or decide on a course of action. They could not answer my technical questions. They usually had to call the factory. However, they were always good for buying you lunch.

Which sales approach was the most successful? It is easy for me to understand the value of a Challenger salesperson when I envision the concept from the perspective of a customer interested in creating a top performing product or service.

Many CEOs worry about people in their organizations who make purchasing decisions based on the perks they get from relationship-building salespeople. For most, it is common sense that buying decisions be based on what is a good business decision, not personal benefit.

I worked for one company, however, that became very proactive and made it a written policy to limit gifts from suppliers to incidental amounts. Lunch or dinner might be ok, but not vacations, cars, or other large gifts.

In one of my other assignments, the company where I worked was spending about $50 million on a factory expansion. Soon after they awarded all the contracts for construction, the lead facilities engineer for the project showed up one day driving the Lincoln Continental previously owned by the general contractor.

Even if this was an innocent, arms-length transaction, the perceptions created should have been enough to nix the deal.

As the leader in your business, how do you want people in your company to make decisions? Moreover, how do you think your customer counterpart wants their employees to make decisions?

Challenger Content is Neutral

What if you do not agree with a focus on building a Challenger sales organization? If you or your organization has a background another selling profile, you might find it difficult to change your approach to sales.

It should not matter to your marketing content. All profiles can receive help from a customer teaching approach to your social media content. You hurt no one by this approach.

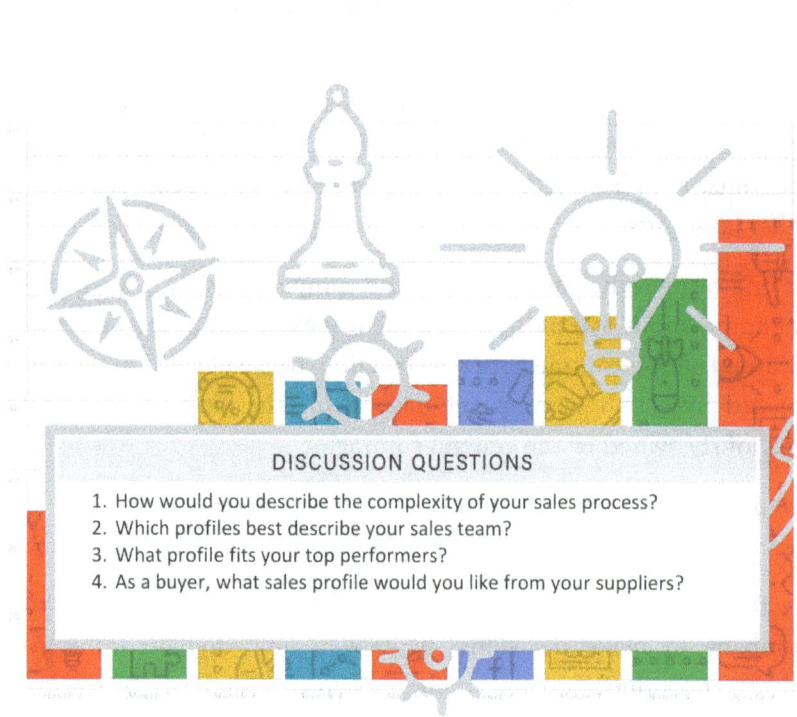

DISCUSSION QUESTIONS

1. How would you describe the complexity of your sales process?
2. Which profiles best describe your sales team?
3. What profile fits your top performers?
4. As a buyer, what sales profile would you like from your suppliers?

IS PATIENCE A VIRTUE?

D o you have patience? Chapter ii named key takeaways from *The Challenger Sale* by Dixon and Adamson, particularly the profile most likely to create a top performer, the Challenger, and the value of a top performer.

Another takeaway for me after reading the book, is the authors belief the conversion to a challenger-selling model is a problem solved within the confines of the sales department. They suggest it might take years for some organizations to change their sales approach to Challenger selling[1].

As a CEO owner founder coach, I cannot recommend you have years of patience. Nor do I agree the issue is solely a sales department issue.

Setting Deadlines

A favorite mentor in my past told me the test period for a general manager was about eighteen months. At that point, you would know what you have, whether the person was going to make it or not.

Similarly, when a venture capital firm invests in a start-up, the funds typically last about eighteen months. A founding CEO expects to show meaningful results by the twelve month point and then spend six months doing another round of fund raising using the evidence from the initial twelve months to justify continued investment.

I can personally attest. For over thirty years in my career, I had either a new boss or a new assignment, every eighteen months.

There is something remarkably familiar about the eighteen-month business breathing cycle.

I believe the same advice should apply to the transformation of your sales culture. You should be able to execute most of the meaningful changes in eighteen months' time.

Dixon and Adamson might be correct with their multi-year viewpoint *if* the leadership of the sales team solely drives change. What would be necessary to accelerate change? Read on.

The Power of Top Executive Leadership

As in all efforts to drive change in an organization, the role of the CEO, owner, or founder is crucial to success.

The first obligation for the top executive is to staff their marketing and sales leadership positions with people intellectually and emotionally aligned with the direction the CEO wishes to pursue. The make-up of the team is the responsibility of the CEO. They are responsible to determine the choice of their next level reports and the retention of the same.

Misalignment is a sure way to fail, a sure way for *any* initiative to fail.

The second obligation is to give public, persistent support to the marketing and sales leadership. As in raising children, there should be no daylight showing between the opinions of mom and dad.

In my first position in general management, I did not realize the power attached to the position. With some experience and some mistakes, I came to understand how subordinates reacted to things I might say or do.

People in your organization emulate what you do. Some do it because they want to please you. Others do it to avoid getting into trouble. Some people see it as a means for career advancement and pay raises.

No matter the motive, your role as the top leader is more influential than you might realize. I had to learn not to think out loud. I did this a couple of times and people took it as direction when I only meant it to be brainstorming.

Managing Your Powers of Influence

There is always momentum to past decisions. People in your organization will find ways to push back on change. This is especially true if your communication comes across as soft and indecisive about an issue.

Persistence is a sure way to deal with change pushback.

Job One

Hire the right people into leadership positions

Job Two

Openly, persistently support those you hire

FIGURE 18. The role of the top executive in driving change.

When your team observes you repeatedly focusing on an issue, they soon learn its importance to you. If you mention something in passing and do not persist, they take it to mean the issue has less priority than other things where you spend a lot of time.

The top executive behavior that would most concern me is indifference to marketing and sales initiatives. I have worked in companies where the top executive remained personally passive to the efforts of their marketing and sales organizations.

I remember one situation where the new president of our company

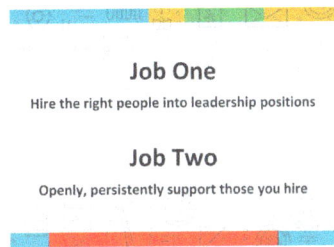

put his desk smack in the middle of the marketing and sales departments soon after he joined the company.

His predecessors treated marketing and sales passively and the marketing and sales teams were used to working without direction from the top. It was a culture shock for them to learn the new president assumed the responsibility and authority to give direction to their organizations.

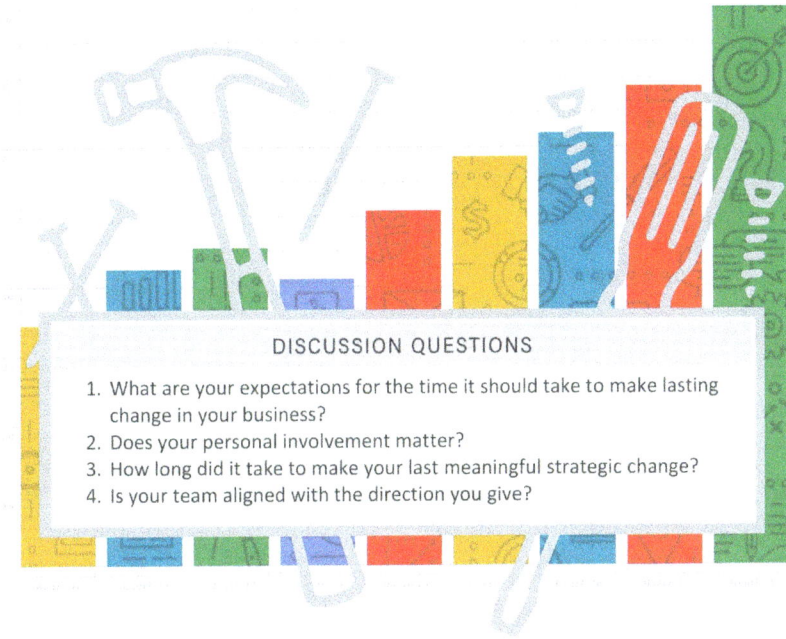

DISCUSSION QUESTIONS

1. What are your expectations for the time it should take to make lasting change in your business?
2. Does your personal involvement matter?
3. How long did it take to make your last meaningful strategic change?
4. Is your team aligned with the direction you give?

14

THE RIGHT TOOL FOR THE JOB

Creating a Challenger marketing and sales effort in your business is not an easy task. Chapter 13 suggested two key things a CEO should do to implement a Challenger marketing and sales team in their organization:

1) Employ the right people, and

2) Persistently support them.

In the last parts of *The Challenger Sale* by Dixon and Adamson, they discuss the nature of the leaders who make successful Challenger sales managers. They cite management skills such as integrity, reliability, and listening skills as necessary traits as these are important in any management position, not just sales management[1].

Candidate Selection is the First Step

If you are creating or expanding your Challenger sales team, you need to be concerned about the people you hire. I am an enthusiastic fan of psychological testing in a hiring process. This is especially true for a critical hire.

At the risk of showing my age, I will confess to you the first testing process I ever used was a test intended for the choice of officers in World War II (Yes, it was old). I knew it as the Stevens-Thoreau Test.

World War II was a time when a team had to scale rapidly, and the military relied on a testing process to select leadership. The other choice was much worse. In terms that might be used by Strategyzer[2], testing had a strong value proposition.

Compared to testing products available on the market today, it was simplistic. The company where I worked used the same test for all management positions. There was no variation in the test for engineers, salespeople, accountants, or managers in operations. All took the same test.

My role at the time was to manage engineers. After a few uses of the tool, I came to realize the best candidates for me had high intelligence (above 90th percentile), and decisiveness (which I associated with getting things done). What did not matter very much was introversion versus extroversion and social ability unless it was at either the end of the scale.

Not everyone in my company agreed with the test or the testing process, usually because they did not like their own scores. This is a point to remember. Nevertheless, my opinion developed through experience was supportive.

One form of criticism was a reliance on the test might result in a manager discarding a candidate that might otherwise be a fit. In other words, it could lead to a false negative; I agree that outcome was a possibility.

My experience was the test never gave me a false positive. I had a high correlation between test results, and high performing employees.

Today's Tests Are Based on Better Science

I have test recommendations for you to consider as you develop your marketing and sales teams: PXT Select[3] from Wylie, HireSelect[4] from Criteria, and SmoothHiring[5] from ClearFit.

Do your diligence on the tests you select. Some tests, for example DISC[6] and Myers-Briggs[7], may give insight into behaviors but they do not get down to the specifics about which candidate you should, or should not hire.

The science for my suggestions is solid. They test for personality traits and interests. I do not recommend testing online for intelligence or cognitive ability unless the test is timed. It is too easy to look up the answers you need. If you want to test for this, you should do it on-site where you can control the environment.

PXT Select distributes through partners who aid you with the mechanics of the test and interpretation. Not only do you get an assessment, you also get interview questions based on the results to help you confirm the results of the test. Uniquely, it also provides recommendations about how to interpret the answers you might get to the questions.

If you test the key people in your organization, you can develop a composite score for the culture of your company. The fit for a candidate might be because the match your existing culture.

Another way to look at fit is if you would like to change your composite score. They could be an addition to your team, which serves to improve your culture.

Typically, users use the test to choose between two or three final candidates in a search process. You pay for each test taken.

HireSelect is a SaaS product. You pay an annual subscription that allows unlimited testing.

SmoothHiring is also a SaaS product. Rather than test final

candidates, the test occupies the beginning of the search process. The application helps you to develop job descriptions and then places the search on all the job-posting boards you wish. Everyone who applies takes the test. The system charges a flat fee per posting , no matter how many candidates take the test, or how many people you intend to hire.

The app then recommends which candidates are the closest fit to your desired candidate profile. Said another way, this tool aids you to screen, unbiasedly, the surge of applications so typical in many searches.

All these suggested products come with standard profiles for typical positions.

Customization

If you want to build a Challenger team, I recommend considering a custom assessment profile rather than the standard profile. With all the suggested testing products, you can develop custom assessment profiles.

There are two ways to do this. You can manually create the profile. However, if you know you already have a good sample of Challengers in your organization that represent top producers, you can test them and let their composite scores serve as your template.

If you have not used testing in hiring before, I recommend you get help to begin. Many small and medium-size businesses are not familiar with testing.

A benefit for creating a custom assessment profile is it causes you to consider your desired profile and allows you to adjust later if necessary.

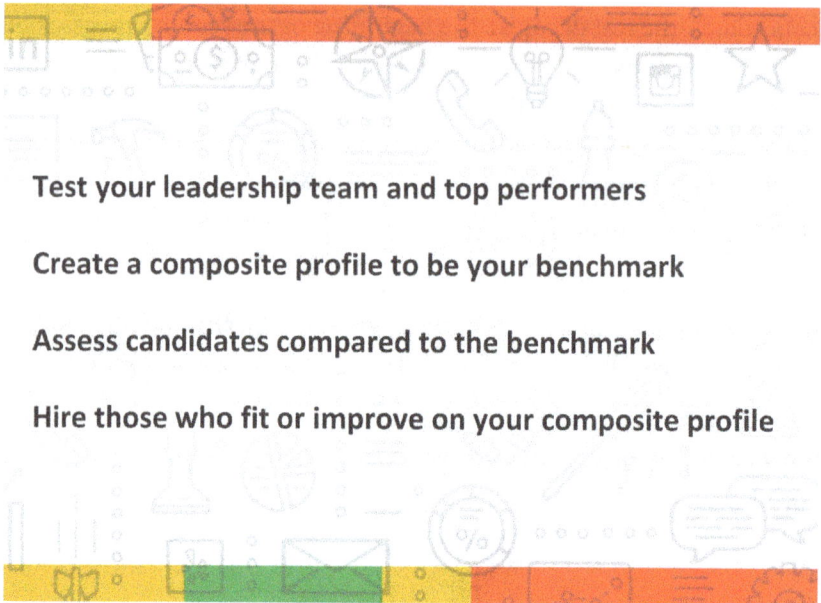

Test your leadership team and top performers

Create a composite profile to be your benchmark

Assess candidates compared to the benchmark

Hire those who fit or improve on your composite profile

FIGURE 19. A custom profile is a way to improve your profile.

Kissing Frogs

You will find most of the applicants you consider are not a fit to your desired profile. Especially when unemployment is low, you may be tempted to compromise on your criteria just to fill an open position.

Your human resources team will feel the competing pressures. On one hand, they know you are eager to get a position filled. On the other hand, they know you want candidates that are a strong fit to the requirements of the position.

Conventional wisdom in a candidate selection process relies on filters that may not completely align with your goals. Some human resource departments discard candidates for reasons like insufficient education or lack of industry experience.

Over-Reliance on Testing

The experts in testing will tell you that there are limitations to testing. For example, in addition to the test results, PXT Select will provide you specific questions and desired answers you can use in your face to face interviews. These assist you to validate the results shown in the test.

Do not use testing as a substitute for other things you do in an interview process. Let your own interviews and instincts play a role. Consider background checks, reference checks, and a review of social media. An on-site cognitive ability test could be useful in your assessment.

I had a colleague in a sales management role who did credit checks on candidates. This might seem counter-intuitive, but he liked candidates with debt. He knew if they needed the money their situation might serve to motivate for success in the job.

If you conduct an interview process without testing, you may also want to remain aware of the fact that candidates who profile as Relationship Builders will work to build a relationship with you. You will find them to be likable and pleasant, but not necessarily qualified.

Onboarding

What you do after you hire a candidate may be as important as the selection process.

If you are building a Challenger team, then knowledge about your products, terms and conditions, pricing, online content, and industry is essential. Challenger sales teams strive to be the most knowledgeable in their industry, something you cannot fake.

Your top marketing and sales people must be good managers and mentors if they want to teach the teachers. The best practices for onboarding begin with a plan. What can you do on the first day? What can you do the first week or the first month? What is the measure of success for onboarding? How do you train, test, and evaluate people in the onboarding process?

How do you decide someone you hired is not a fit? Do you have a staged onboarding process? Does a new hire need to master one stage before they go to the next?

DISCUSSION QUESTIONS

1. What is your process for making key hiring decisions?
2. How do you decide the criteria to use for hiring?
3. Do you know the profiles for your existing team?
4. How do you assess fit with your organization?

15

A CHALLENGE FOR THE LEADER

This might be a what-came-first, the-chicken-or-the-egg issue. Can someone who is not an effective mentor create a mentoring organization?

Does building a Challenger sales team affect the way you lead?

Chapter 13 discussed ways you could build a Challenger sales team starting with ways to recruit and select candidates for your team. Selection, however, is the beginning of the leadership process, not the end.

Your chances for being successful leading a challenger sales team depend, in part, on a personal self-assessment of leader you want to be.

Leading a Challenger Team

If you are leading a Challenger team, you serve best if you see your role as a mentor and teacher. You are teaching the teachers in your organization. To improve performance, create top performers, mentor, and coach.

Are you uncomfortable to see yourself as a mentor?

If you reflect on the people who were most helpful to your career, you would associate descriptions like patient, honest, straightforward, wise, trustworthy, sharing, calm, respected, and thoughtful. As a mentor, you want to act like the people who mentored you.

There are also people you have met who represent the way you *do not* want to be. These are also influential to your behavior, albeit in a negative way. Your descriptions might include terms such as devious, political, self-centered, brutal, backstabbing, bullying, evil, and manipulative.

Building a challenger organization might be a way for you to enjoy your business life because you like mentoring and like to see others build their skills and enjoy results.

Leading Other Types of Teams

With the other profiles identified in *The Challenger Sale*; Hard Worker, Relationship Builder, Reactive Problem Solver, and Lone Wolf, your means to improve your team's performance is likely to be built on a system for judging people[1].

If you want more sales per salesperson, you need to keep your best and free up the future for the bottom performers. You emphasize quotas and rank people for determining retention. If you manage in this fashion, you are building your team around people, not around process. You are also building a stressful work environment.

One of the most painful moments I saw was a time where we had a meeting with a CAD software company interested to secure our business. We had about ten people from our company in attendance. A salesperson and sales manager attended from the software company.

For one easily forgettable reason or another, the senior person from the software company berated his employee in our meeting. This was completely at odds with my managerial sensibilities.

Not only do you not criticize an employee in public, you should never do it in front of customers, especially a large group.

I learned later the software company had extremely high employee turnover with an industry reputation for creating a high-stress sales culture. Did they make a sale to my company? Not a chance, I quickly ended the meeting and ushered them from the building.

Before you jump to conclusions, I am not suggesting you should not judge performance. It is important to be aware of how people are serving the business. Some simply may not be a fit. However, if you devote most of your time to judging and little time to mentoring, I believe you will not have much success to develop top performers.

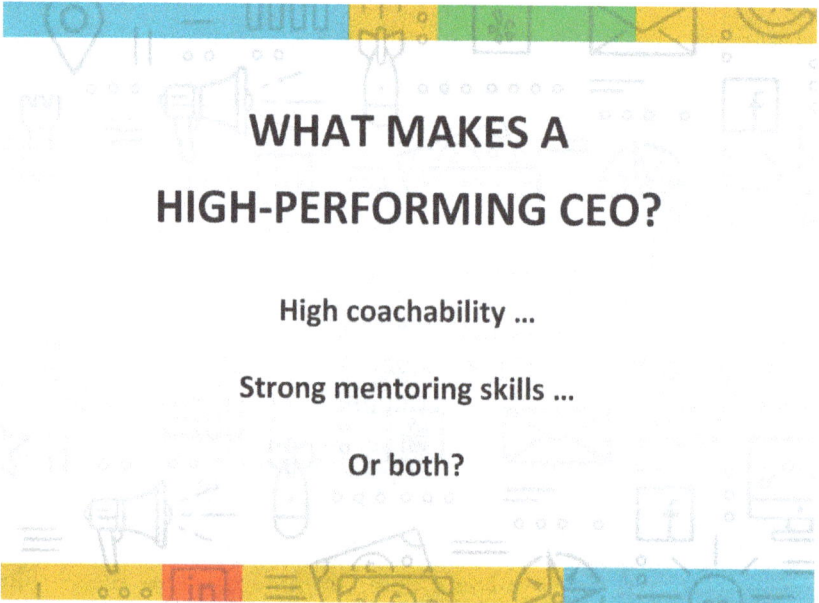

WHAT MAKES A HIGH-PERFORMING CEO?

High coachability ...

Strong mentoring skills ...

Or both?

FIGURE 20. Do mentored leaders pay it forward?

Wise People, Foolish People, and Evil People

Psychologist Henry Cloud divides the world into three types of people, Wise, Foolish, and Evil[2]. I believe this concept can apply to the concept of building challenger teams.

Wise people are open to feedback. They are coachable, and a mentor enjoys working with them. When you suggest an alternative to consider, they appreciate it. I would make the assertion that wise people make the best Challenger sales people. They like to mentor and receive mentoring; to coach and receive coaching.

Foolish people make excuses. They resist feedback and seldom admit to a mistake. To manage these people, you must set strong boundaries to their behaviors and explain to them the process. These people are frustrating to a mentor because the mentor usually cannot see progress.

As noted previously, if your selection process includes testing, the coachability score might be *critical* in your decision-making.

Evil people are those who want to hurt others. If you sense this personality in your organization, you should act at once to protect yourself and your organization; no questions asked. These situations often need legal help.

What was the sales manager from the CAD software company? He classifies as Evil. If he was in my company, his future would be free very soon.

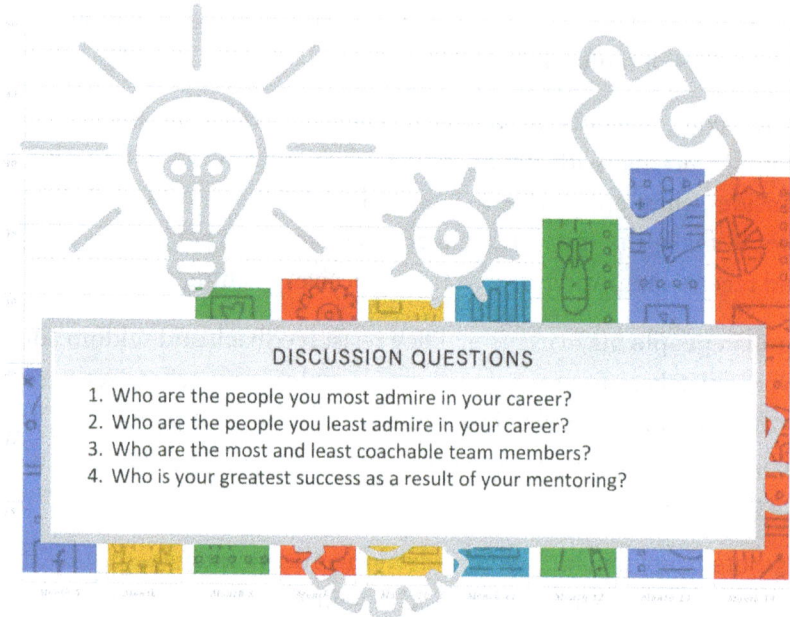

DISCUSSION QUESTIONS

1. Who are the people you most admire in your career?
2. Who are the people you least admire in your career?
3. Who are the most and least coachable team members?
4. Who is your greatest success as a result of your mentoring?

16

LEADERS NEED FOLLOWERS

Organizational development is important at all levels, not just for your team leaders. Chapter 14 discussed ways to find and select people who are strong fit for your team. Is selection and hiring all you need to do? Is management that simple?

Why Selection? Why Training?

People seldom make lasting changes in their personality. At best, they can shift their behaviors slightly, if they are aware their performance could improve with a shift. When we are building teams and desiring team members who are coachable, we must use selection processes to get what we want.

Training cannot improve manageability, energy levels, and decisiveness, for example. Name these traits in the selection process. Likewise, we all have interests built in to our profiles.

Training is useful for technical knowledge about your products or services, terms and conditions of sale or services, company policies, frequently asked questions and other forms of company-specific content.

You have seen job postings where hiring managers look for industry experience. Do they really seek knowledge that training could be doing or are they really asking for someone who can bring a contact list? Would it be better to hire by focusing on the personality traits you want?

Training to Sell

You can train sales skills. If you have selected for the right personality traits, there might still be a gap in the knowledge about how to sell.

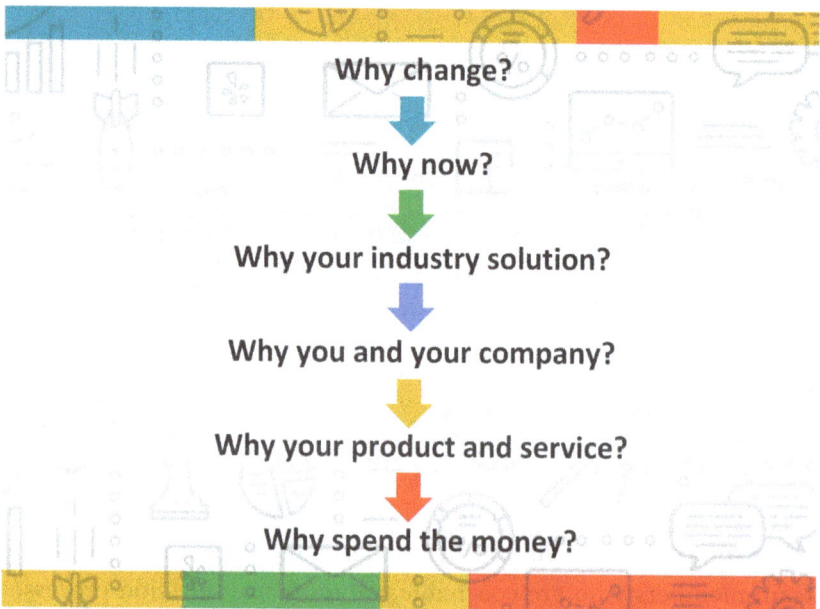

Why change?

Why now?

Why your industry solution?

Why you and your company?

Why your product and service?

Why spend the money?

FIGURE 21. Sales process sequence. Adapted from Hoffeld.

The Science of Selling by Hoffeld is an informative read if you want to know more about personal development for salespeople as well as understand the underlying science. Hoffeld suggests there are six steps in a buying decision-making process, which he terms the *six whys*[1] (not to be confused with the 5 *why's* from lean thinking).

Hoffeld draws from several studies into the behaviors of both buyers and sellers.

You can also hire sales trainers. If you search the Hubspot[2] website, you can find a list of twenty-five sales training organizations.

I strongly believe in train-do approaches. If your training is merely a classroom lecture, you will accomplish little. When a hands-on exercise follows a presentation, you enhance the effectiveness of the training. Explore the training process before you select a training company.

Another recommendation is to persist. People benefit from time in the field and return with questions and concerns. Reinforcement is important.

In one company, we had two full-time sales trainers who did nothing but travel with salespeople, especially new people. It was a wise investment as we were managing 125 salespeople and there were always new members on the team.

Another practice that worked well was to have all-hands sales meetings. When I was working in product development, our introductions were so many we had quarterly meetings. While this involved considerable expense, we almost tripled the sales of the company in four years.

This also allowed for peer-to-peer interaction. Sometimes salespeople are skeptical about the potential success of a new process or program.

I once had a colleague who was the vice president of sales who had a strong opinion. His viewpoint was the role of salespeople is to sell, not to buy. More than once, he voiced his opinion to his team. Otherwise a gregarious person, he used a serious tone with this topic.

In another case, a rapidly growing company which was a sister division to mine, considered their sales staffing to be a task critical to their growth. They knew their market share was low and calculated the potential return each incremental sales hire could bring to the company.

To track and review growth, metrics included the size of the sales team and the number of new hires. When discussing company growth, it was in the context of the size of the sales force.

Getting the Story Told the Right Way

Having a proactive training program, whether through meetings and/or field trainers, also lets you dispense some control on the story about your competitive advantage.

Consider the converse situation. If you do not train people, what are they going to say about your company? Are untrained salespeople another way to see sales as a person, not a process?

DISCUSSION QUESTIONS

1. In your company, what skills can be trained and what personality traits must be considered when hiring?
2. What content is in your current sales training efforts?
3. Would additional sales team members grow your sales?
4. What can your salespeople tell you about winning orders?

17

FIVE SIMPLE WAYS TO PERSIST

How do you gauge persistence? If the first role of a CEO is to select the right people, the second role is equally important. Give persistent support to the marketing and sales leadership if you want a lasting shift towards a whole-organization, aligned Challenger sales culture.

Persistence as a tool to drive the pace of change was discussed in Chapter 13. In this chapter, I will dig deeper into more of the subtleties in the practice of using persistence as a leadership tool.

For any desired strategic change, persistence is a proper behavior for a top executive.

This comment begs a follow-on question, however. What does persistent support look like?

Talk about it in every interaction. Be relentless. Make it important.

Seek feedback from your organization. Ask questions about the topic.

Always consult with your sales and marketing leadership before any tactical pivot.

Align your compensation plans. You get what you pay for.

Compliment people when you see good things happen. Say "thank you".

FIGURE 22. Senior executives drive meaningful change.

Do Not Ever Give Up

Driving change or giving strategic direction in an organization needs consistency on the part of leadership, especially if there is a meaningful change from the way it's always been done.

Top executive influence was proven to me clearly, when I had the opportunity to serve on a corporate safety committee. My company had about twenty-five manufacturing facilities. It was fascinating to me to learn that about 80 percent of the accidents occurred in 20 percent of the facilities.

The difference between the performing and non-performing facilities was the attitude and support given to the program by the top executive at each location. Because the content in the program was constant, it was clear the difference was the leader.

Why Does Persistence Make an Issue Important?

Personal Commitment. More than anything else, persistence shows your personal commitment to the change. Demonstrate your knowledge and be articulate. Put in extra hours to accommodate the change process.

Remember, you are on stage with your organization.

Relative Importance. Persistence shows the ranking you give it compared to other issues that might be in the business.

You should have awareness about your personal focus. Your organization senses the importance of issues. If you unintentionally drift in another direction, they will follow you.

Consider the other extreme. If you mention it only occasionally, do you think people in your organization will consider it important? Will they focus on other goals?

Simplicity. It does not cost you anything to manage your behavior or the way you dispense leadership. You need not hire a consultant, use a public relations firm, hire anybody, or purchase anything.

You need to make it your agenda.

Consistency. How many times have you heard the trite term, "flavor of the month," when employees discuss the leadership they are seeing?

Persistence is the antidote to cure this viewpoint. There are people in your organization that will fade into the background waiting to learn whether change will stick.

For me, these people are the most frustrating. Their behavior is passive aggressive. Your job as the senior executive is to grind them into alignment.

Honest Disagreement

Suppose one of your subordinates does not agree with a change you suggest for the company. Suppose they truly oppose your thinking and you notice your persistence is not having an effect.

I suggest you try to have an adult conversation with them to put the issue squarely in front of both of you. It might be best if they pursued employment elsewhere. The situation is stressful for them and the misalignment in thinking is damaging to your organization.

Work out an exit plan for them.

Sometimes confronting the issue directly will get them on board with the direction you want to go. They may have to weigh all the consequences of their behavior and make a choice. If you allow for them to make a choice, be sure you think this through beforehand. Some employees are expert survivors. You do not want continued passive resistance, you want change.

At the very least, set some clear goals for them which demonstrate allegiance to your change. Be sure your measures are simple and have short deadlines.

DISCUSSION QUESTIONS

1. On what issue did you recently spend the most time?
2. Is there an issue where your team just "doesn't get it"?
3. Do people in your company discuss the "flavor of the month"?
4. What is the way you get feedback about your leadership?

COMFORT IS THE LACK OF DISCOMFORT

For those who understand ergonomics, comfort is defined as the lack of discomfort. Product design practitioners knowledgeable about ergonomics know that you create discomfort when you place too much weight at too small a point.

It creates a hot spot which compels you to shift in your chair or toss and turn on your mattress. Too much time with your arms unsupported over a keyboard creates neck pains. You achieve comfort when you uniformly support the human body.

I see an analogy in the way to understand operational customer support issues in business marketing and sales efforts. Chapter 11 mentioned the importance of operational customer experience issues. This chapter will expand on the topic.

The surest way to undermine your best-laid marketing and sales efforts is to create hot spots and pain points in your customer experience.

One way to create a great customer experience is to end bad customer experience. Likewise, you can act to motivate salespeople by removing things that de-motivate salespeople.

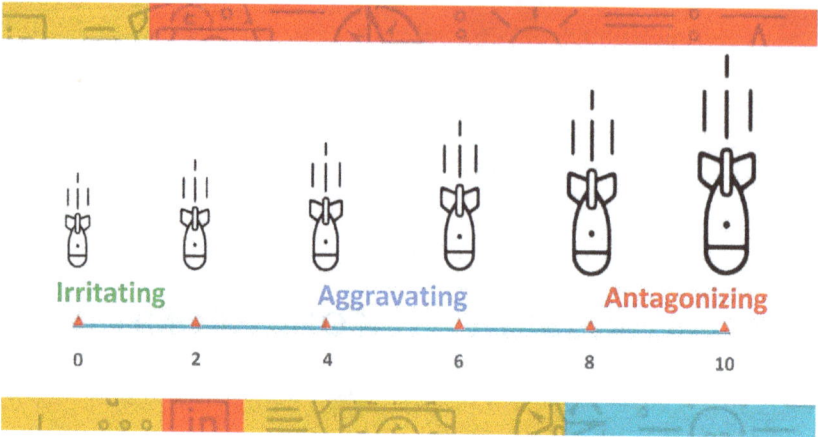

FIGURE 23. Can you measure customer pain in megatons?

The Importance of Quality

High-performing CEOs understand the fundamentals about quality management. The first fundamental to understand is the importance of quality management. Here are a few reasons quality is important.

Sales Performance. Think of salespeople as the promise makers for your business. They interact with your customers who ask many questions. The best salespeople are responsive. It is extremely hard and very demoralizing for them to promise something and then have your company operations do otherwise.

If you want a top-performing Challenger sales team, you must consider yourself to be responsible as the chief salesperson and do what you must to motivate salespeople.

Customer Retention. For almost any business, the future value of a customer is greater than the present value of an order. Doing what it takes to ensure a quality experience should be common sense.

In most businesses, there is a switching cost for a buyer. A switching cost can include direct costs but there is also an emotional side to switching. Most people have an aversion to change if their current practice is not creating pain points.

Defects in your products, services, or customer experience are pain points for your customers. If these are chronic and persist, your customers will be open to switching to the way they did things before you were a supplier, or to your competitor. Said another way, in their assessment, your pain point is a greater cost than their switching cost.

On the other hand, if you are acting to remove pain points, you are not just helping yourself; you are making the switching costs for your competitor higher.

Cost. The cost of a quality defect is far more that the value of the associated transaction. There are opportunity costs. If your resources, time and money, are spent on fixing issues on the surface you are working on a non-value-added activity rather than something which might advance the growth or profitability of your company.

Naming Customer Experience Hot Spots

How does a CEO know which issues matter the most and where to deploy corrective action?

A common process for finding customer experience issues is Pareto Analysis[1]. Pareto Analysis is a basic quality assurance tool. Experienced practitioners record and categorize defects.

For discussion, the defects could be product defects, service defects, or customer experience defects. A defect is any occurrence that does not meet the specifications of the product or service.

Some people view high quality as products with many features, or luxury goods. In the world of quality management, high quality is not about luxury features. High quality occurs when the number of defects is low when compared to the number of opportunities for defects to occur.

Periodically (usually monthly, could be weekly), the data on defects is summarized and ranked. Quality assurance professionals express the results by calculating the frequency which occurrences occur in parts per million, or PPM.

For example, if you shipped to the wrong address ten times out of 1,000 shipments, you would have 10,000 PPM as a defect rate for shipping address accuracy. If you measure your performance as 99 percent, your corresponding defect rate would be 10,000 PPM. Using the PPM metric brings focus to occurrences of defects, in contrast to a percentage correct measure that seems to be more about buzz and bragging rights than a sincere interest in improvement.

The denominator in this calculation could be the total number of products shipped or orders fulfilled or transactions. Pick a metric that most people in your company will understand.

To add more sophistication to your process, you could also calculate or estimate the cost for the defect to the customer. This might be a better way to measure pain. A low frequency but high-cost defect might be more important to solve than a high frequency but low-cost defect.

The defects with the highest PPM, or PPM times cost, are the ones which demand corrective action from top management.

Why CEOs Do not Fix Defects

There is nothing new about Pareto Analysis and it is not a complex activity. I see many companies, however, which do not employ the practice. The leadership team gives lip service to quality but in practice do not execute on many simple practices.

Some leaders react by doing inspection as a substitute for fixing defects. I am not against inspection practices, per se, but I do not see it as an activity that solves root cause issues. Frankly, inspection adds no lasting value to what you do. It might prevent an immediate issue, but you should not view it as a substitute for real problem solving.

I have also seen some creative and effective ways to manage quality. I know one company who put the prioritization of quality issues in the hands of the customer service people in their organization. The head of customer service chaired the monthly meeting and could speak eloquently to relate what customers were saying about the issues.

No matter how you execute your quality program, remember one of the key roles of a CEO is to give air cover to the subordinate acting as the guru for your quality management system.

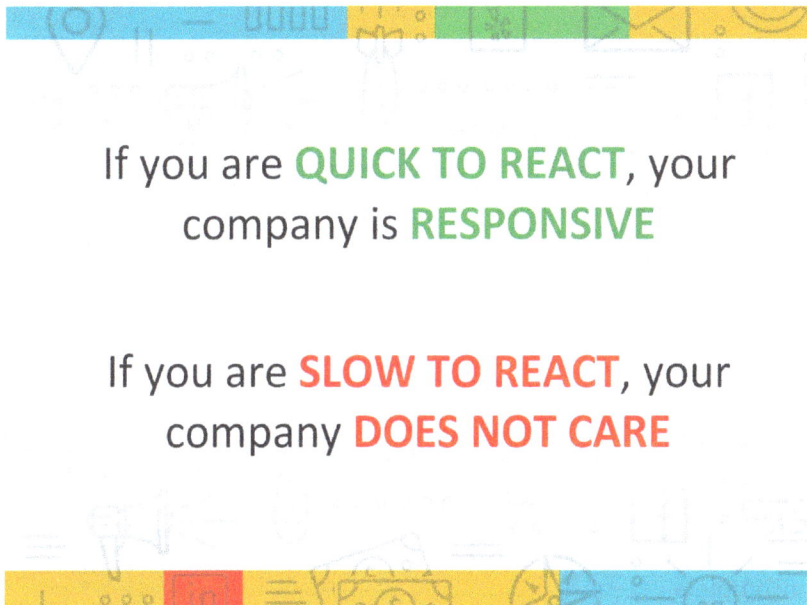

If you are **QUICK TO REACT**, your company is **RESPONSIVE**

If you are **SLOW TO REACT**, your company **DOES NOT CARE**

FIGURE 24. Is your company responsive or a company that does not care?

Hero or Villain?

The time you take to respond to a customer quality issue makes a difference in the way customers perceive you.

If you can solve an issue in a day or two, the customer sees your company as one that is responsive, caring about the needs of customers, and well-managed. If you solve the same issue days or weeks later, or never at all, the customer will see your company as uncaring, disinterested, disorganized, and poorly managed.

They are right ... your company is uncaring, disinterested, disorganized, and poorly managed.

When discussing your improvement priorities in your quality management meetings, take into consideration the time a quality defect has existed in your business. A chronic issue might cumulatively aggravate your customers.

A Source for Content

When you make a change to improve the quality of your products, services, or customer experience, trumpeting the change to your target market is important.

You can include it in a blog post, social media message, and newsletter. The event makes excellent content to all the external and internal constituencies discussed in chapter 9.

Frequent Updates for Frequently Asked Questions

Many companies include an FAQ or frequently asked questions page in their website designs. Most are moderately useful and usually incomplete.

If the questions asked and answered serve to educate your customer, I agree this is excellent content.

If the questions asked and answered explain a work-around to an issue you have, or include a lengthy how-to, you are just covering for a bad customer experience design in your process.

If customers ask a question often, could this be a place you might innovate on your customer experience?

Also, reflect on who has the responsibility in your company for managing the FAQ's. When you built your website, did you add an associated content management system to keep the FAQs current and relevant?

DISCUSSION QUESTIONS

1. What are the ways you measure quality?
2. Do you have chronic quality issues?
3. What is your company's response time to resolve quality issues?
4. How do you communicate quality improvements made by your company to your customers?

19

CREATE DEMAND, TURN DEMAND INTO REVENUE

P revious chapters refer to marketing and sales as a single thought. A part of this was deliberate to impress upon you the importance of alignment between organizations.

However, there is a difference. Marketing creates demand. Sales turns demand into revenues by leading customers through the buying process.

Marketing Alone Will Not Grow Revenues

In my discussions with marketers and business leaders, I often note a false expectation. Many business leaders invest in new websites, search engine optimization (SEO) services, social media campaigns, and other fashionable and effective marketing tools expecting these to grow sales. A few months later, they sense no progress.

If the marketing programs grow awareness about your value proposition, enhance your customer experience, name the right target customers, and teach your customers about their businesses, is there a reason you cannot see increases in revenues?

Most often, these leaders confuse marketing with sales.

I saw a dramatic example. I started a new position where I handled marketing and sales to a customer segment that was identifiable and large.

Not long after I started, I learned we had over 300 leads accumulated from the previous year. The typical revenue for each closed sale was at least $250,000. Sadly, no one was following up on the leads.

Marketing had specific names and contact information for projects that were active. The company paid for presence at a trade show and collected many leads. Very few leads were unfit for our business model.

No one bothered to tabulate or assign the leads. There was nothing wrong with the other parts of the process. When following a lead, we had a good close rate. Our ratio of revenue to customer acquisition cost was about ten to one.

The breakdown in the process was the hand-off of leads from marketing to sales.

The remedy was not complicated. We started to insist on entering every lead into a customer relationship management system, assigning it to a specific salesperson that was responsible and accountable, held recurring progress review meetings, and added headcount to the sales staff.

Revenues grew the following year by over 40 percent.

If You Invest in Marketing, Invest in Sales

A high-performing CEO understands the value of keeping a balance in the resources devoted to marketing and sales. A lead that goes without sales follow-up is as bad as a salesperson without a lead assigned.

Some business leaders are inattentive to this part of the process. They do not ask to have leads tabulated, ignore resources, and budget levels, and do not trust their sales-closing processes to function repeatedly.

If You Invest in Sales, Invest in Marketing

Hiring salespeople without an active marketing function is a way for you to create a Lone Wolf selling organization. You are leaving it up to the salespeople to name their own customer segments and find their own leads.

You lose control of the metrics. You will not know who a lead is, how many leads you have, or whether leads are growing in number over earlier periods.

The expense you save by avoiding marketing efforts will be a pittance compared to opportunities lost in an unmanaged process.

Why do marketing and sales efforts get out of balance?

No tracking system for leads

Inadequate marketing resources

Inadequate sales resources

Lack of confidence in sales closing processes

Management inattention

FIGURE 25. *Keep efforts in balance to avoid wasting resources.*

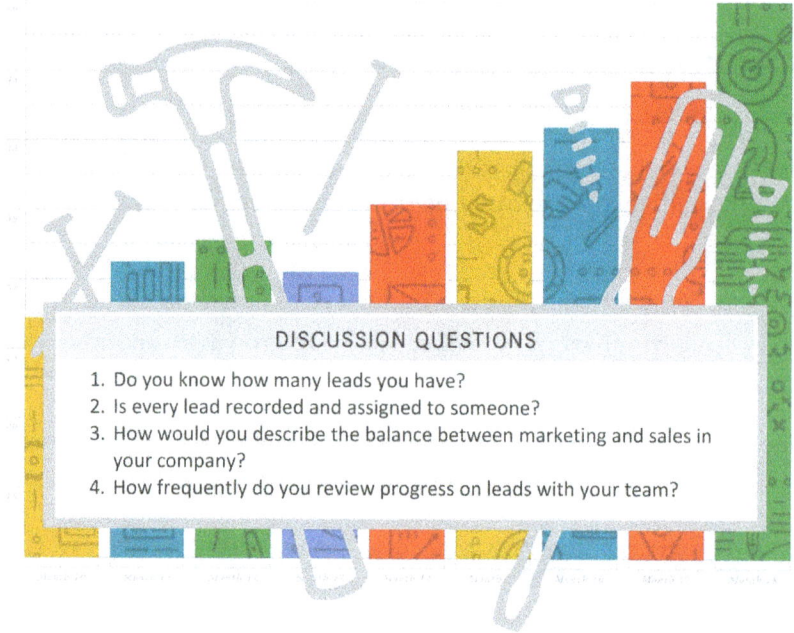

DISCUSSION QUESTIONS

1. Do you know how many leads you have?
2. Is every lead recorded and assigned to someone?
3. How would you describe the balance between marketing and sales in your company?
4. How frequently do you review progress on leads with your team?

20

THE CASE FOR SPENDING ON MARKETING

Keeping a balance between your investments in marketing and sales is important, as noted in chapter 17. Some businesses, however, do not distinguish between the two and expect the sales staff to do marketing. This may have been a useful approach but in a business environment where online marketing is more important, skills other than selling might be more relevant.

How and where should you spend on marketing? Here are thoughts to consider.

Put Online Content First

Nobody has an unlimited budget. Since funds are limited, how to spend them?

I have seen many practices. I know of cases where marketers decided to do a little bit of everything in planning their campaigns. Brochures, trade shows, speaking engagements, social media campaigns, paid online ads, blogs, email campaigns; all of these and others could be useful.

I can endorse this strategy if you do not know what will work for your business when you are starting up or when your results fade. You might have assumptions in your business model about the ways you reach customers. Validate and re-validate these periodically.

For a marketing leader in a more mature business, I do not understand why they might champion the do-everything logic. Is there a fear you could miss something? Do they want to avoid conflict in the event a peer or boss suggests they did not do all they could do? Did they wish to be thorough?

At some point, you need to put metrics in place, so you know what works for you.

In other cases, the status quo seems to prevail. We "spent x on y last year and this year plan to spend ..." seems another way to avoid perceived risk. Can someone accuse you of taking unnecessary chances if you do it the same way?

If you lead a small or medium-size business, you may not have the resources or means to clearly assess the effectiveness of various marketing approaches. You may be in the trap of doing the same things now you did before. If so, then let us cut to the chase.

The Minimum

Few buyers in any industry for any product or service do not investigate your company, your products or services, and you, without going online. Your marketing efforts must give them things to find.

If you do not give them things to find, they will find out about the lack of content too! This is a bad competitive position, especially if your competition's website has more or better content than your website. If you are doing a marketing benchmark study comparing your company to your competition, benchmark the websites.

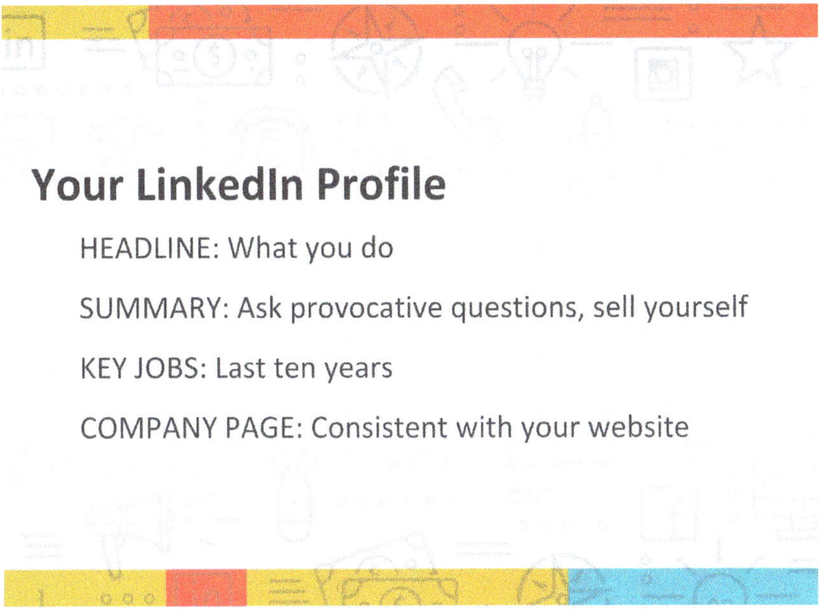

Your LinkedIn Profile

HEADLINE: What you do

SUMMARY: Ask provocative questions, sell yourself

KEY JOBS: Last ten years

COMPANY PAGE: Consistent with your website

FIGURE 26. Your minimum effort for a personal online presence.

At the very least, you should have a professional website which displays properly on all mobile and desktop devices. Your leadership team should have personal profiles on LinkedIn.

The personal profiles should appear similarly in your website and on LinkedIn. While you are at it, create a LinkedIn company page, so viewers of your profile can easily navigate from your LinkedIn company page to your website home page.

The professional website home page should describe the problem you solve and/or the opportunity you have for your target market segment. A stranger who fits your target segment, should easily see him or herself in your presentation and know they should do a deeper dive into your company. This is the page where your readers learn *why* they should do business with you.

Later, when you study your analytics, you will learn this is the most visited page on your website.

Your Company Website

HOME PAGE: Clearly state your value proposition

ABOUT: Key team members, history

PRODUCTS / SERVICES: Short Descriptions

CONTACT: Location, Phone, Email, Hours

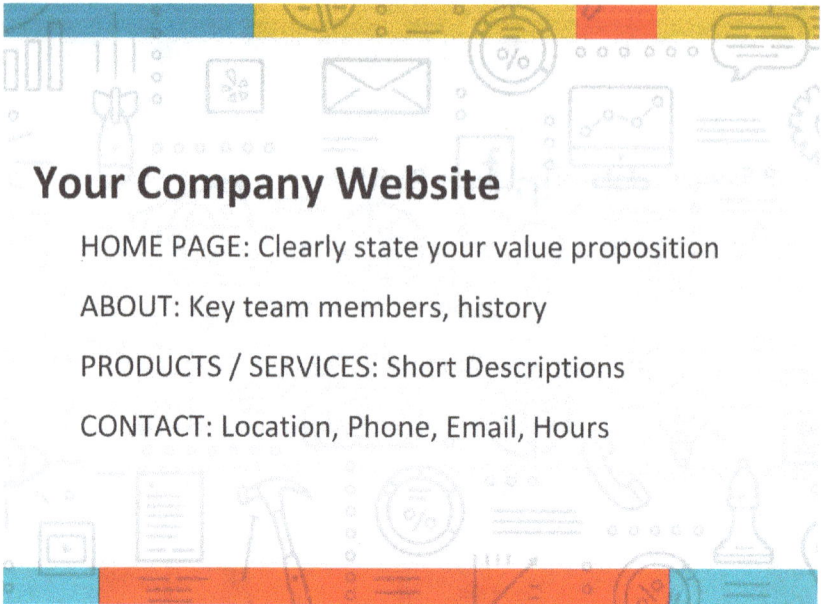

FIGURE 27. Your minimum effort to have a business website.

Your home page should also have a call to action. If visitors would like to learn more about your compelling story, give them a straightforward way to connect with you.

The about page might give a history and profile of your company and information about the key leadership. Give your website visitors a way to prepare themselves for visiting you in person. When you explain your background, make a connection between your career and your current role. A best practice is to write this in first person.

The products or services page should reinforce the message from the home page. This is a good place to explain the scope of your value proposition.

A minimum website should also include a contact page. Make it easy for people to reach out to you. Show maps, addresses, hours, phone numbers.

I also believe that appearance matters. To create the minimum-acceptable website, you should either engage a graphic designer or use a recent template from one of the prominent website builder sites.

In residential real estate, there is the concept of curb appeal. The first impression made becomes a lasting impression. The same is true for your website. Since this is primarily the way people begin their study of your business today, your website is the first impression.

Professional website graphic design also uses many images. Your first choice should be images that come from your business, as these personalize your site. Alternatively, there are many commercially available images. Be sure these are high resolution and free to use and share commercially.

Some readers will ask me to explain my view of a minimum website. My reason is simple. I see many businesses that do not live up to any minimum standards.

You may assume bad websites correlate with tech-challenged business leaders, baby-boomers for example. I also see millennial-created start-up businesses that do not pay attention to this detail.

Before you commit to any website build, be sure you know how to update it. If there is an excessive cost and potential delays, these will be a barrier to change. It is possible to spend as much on change over time as the cost of the site in the beginning. You or someone you assign should be able to make changes to images and script without third party involvement.

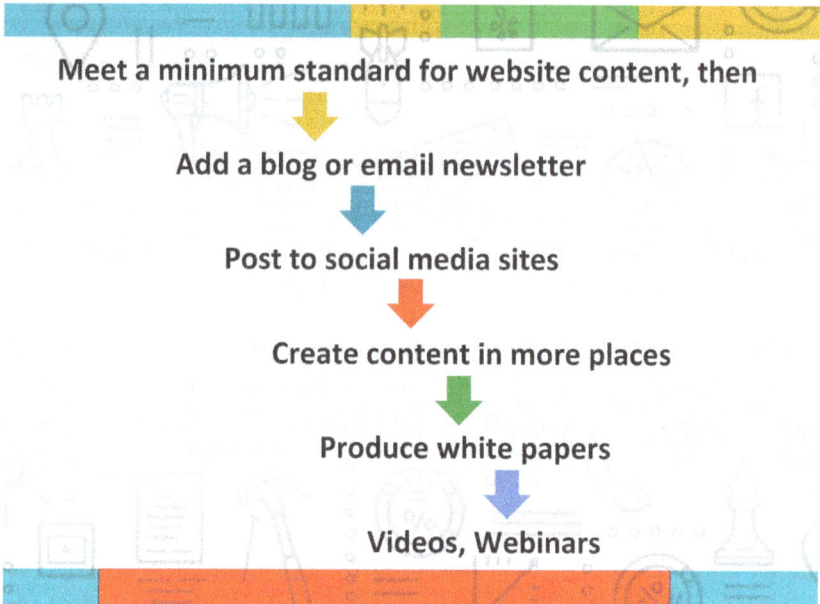

FIGURE 28. Meet the minimum for presence, and then act to create engagement.

If No One Is There

Building your website or creating your personal profile means nothing if no one visits. You have heard the question, "if a tree falls in the forest, and no one is there, does it make a sound?" We should change the question and ask, "If you are online and no one visits, have you done any marketing?"

There is no point in building even a minimal website or creating a LinkedIn profile if you do not pair that with an effort to get people to visit.

If the first level of success is to achieve is to have online content, the next step is to engage your target audiences.

A few things to consider are blogging, email campaigns, video content, and social media posts like tweets. You can also post articles on your LinkedIn company page and do the same on a Facebook page. Then there are paid options like Google Ads[1] and Facebook Ads[2].

The challenge with this step is to create a stream of content.

Blogs, newsletters, and videos are most valuable if they are repetitive and have great content, preferably Challenger content that creates engagement with readers. A stream of frivolous content can lead to potential customers who unsubscribe.

I would recommend you personally contribute minimally to this effort. Delegate the task. You will not have the personal bandwidth to be a content creator.

In some industries, there are services that supply shared content, especially if the industry is fragmented. Examples might be dentists, realtors, attorneys, or car repair shops.

You can also engage an independent writer to create content for you. The downside to this approach is you may find it difficult to find an expert or you must do editing yourself to compensate for a lack of industry knowledge.

The greatest value of blogs and newsletters might not be from the content itself but the opportunity its existence affords. If you are creating content, then you can promote it on social media channels like Facebook, Instagram, LinkedIn, and Twitter.

In my role as an executive coach, my fastest growing clients are the ones who do the best job with their online efforts. I don't believe this is a coincidence.

In my role doing diligence on potential merger and acquisition deals, comparable companies which spend the most on marketing show the most growth and therefore attract the most suitors and highest price multiples.

If you can realize the fastest growth or best price on exit, what is there not to like about online presence and online marketing?

Another way to create engagement is to rely on referrals. An endorsement from an existing customer or a friend to your business is effective when it occurs.

However, referral marketing can also be slow and limited. BNI, an organization devoted to referral marketing, coaches its members that it takes six to nine months of weekly meetings for others to feel comfortable giving you referrals. To get many referrals, you need to do a lot of networking.

Referral marketing is also a tactic that fits with the Relationship Building approach to sales rather than the Challenger approach to sales.

If each unit of sales for your product or service is a small amount, then the net cost of getting a customer through a referral might exceed the desired cost ratio of twenty to one. Conversely, if each referral results in a large amount of revenue, referral marketing should remain one of your tactics.

Before the invention of the internet, referral marketing was a leading way to find potential customers. There were also telemarketing campaigns, radio and TV ads, and in-person sales calls. You could also buy space on a billboard, fly a banner over the stadium, drop leaflets from an airplane, or send a dog with a note in its mouth.

If you cling solely to these approaches, you may be missing much better ways to pitch your product or service.

DISCUSSION QUESTIONS

1. What % of revenues do you devote to marketing?
2. How marketing spending allocated?
3. Do customers search online for your product or service? Do you need to reach out to find customers?
4. If you spent any additional money on marketing, what would you do?

21

CONNECT AND COMPETE

Have you noticed some of the best ideas or products seem simple and elegant? Have you asked yourself, "why didn't I think of that?" Some products just really connect with people.

Do you admire products or services like the Uber app, or the Aeron chair, or the iPhone?

At the other end of the spectrum are products and services that just seem like mush. You do not see value or competitive advantage. Do you spend a lot of time shopping because you have no sense about how to make your choice? Does nothing in the market stand out to you?

Chapter 18 discussed the importance of investing in marketing. If you agree, then your next task is to give direction to your marketing. Can you say what you want your brand to stand for? Do you know what you want all your target customers to associate with your company? Alternatively, why they should do business with you?

Play to Win

In the classic TV game show *Family Feud,* contestants name the word the audience most associates with a topic.

If I said, "name a popular electric car," would the top answer be Tesla? If I said, "name a reliable, low-cost airline," would the top answer be Southwest Airlines? If I said, "name a city in which to gamble," would the top answer be Las Vegas?

You, as a consumer, have a clear association for many brands.

This should be the aim for your company too. Part of your marketing plan should be to create awareness in your customers and cement your reputation in their mind. This happens when you are consistent and persistent with the messaging.

If you do not have a clear plan for your desired company reputation, you have choices.

Another term some use is competitive advantage. What does your company do which is unmatched by any competitor? If you do not know or cannot articulate this, you:

1) do not have competitive advantage, or

2) need help to create the competitive advantage message.

In figure 29, I make a few suggestions for you to consider. This is not a comprehensive list.

EASIEST TO USE: If the current process is complex

EASIEST TO LEARN: If training costs are high or turnover is an issue

MOST FEATURES: If products or services are used many ways

LOWEST COST: If products or services are viewed as a commodity

MOST DURABLE: If investment is high or downtime has a high cost

MOST GREEN: If societal impact is a consideration

MOST LUXURIOUS: If image is the key buying determinant

EASIEST TO MODIFY: If your product or service will be customized

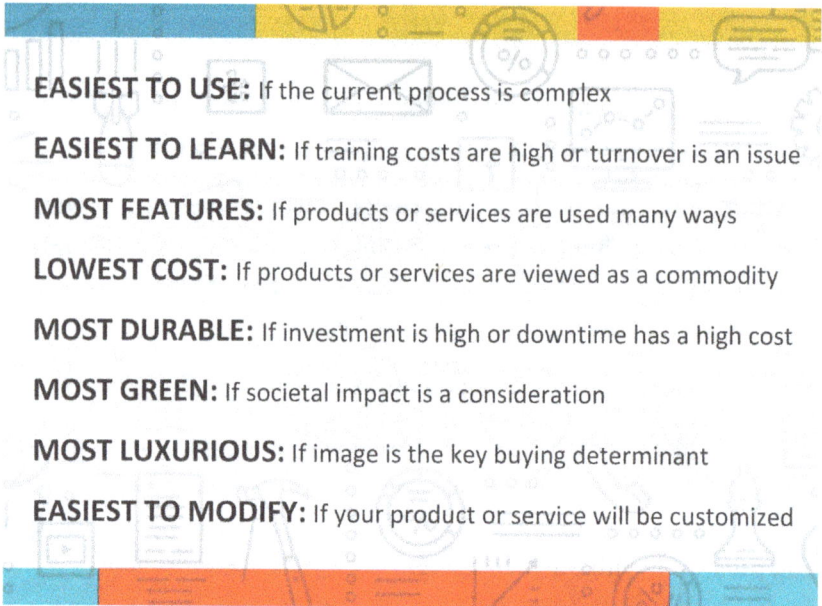

FIGURE 29. Ways to position your company compared to your competition.

Your Brand, Value Proposition, Customer Experience

If you do some study, you will find it easier to decide about desired brand identity.

Study Your Competitors. Who are your competitors? What makes another company a competitor?

They are the other companies considered as alternates by your target customer segment. In some industries, they might be companies that look a lot like you. In today's competitive environment, an online competitor might be important.

Determine your competition by thinking about it from the perspective of your customers. I have met many CEOs who do not really know who much about their competition. They consider too many companies as their competition, not stopping to realize that another company who might do similar things is serving a completely different customer segment.

Once you know which companies you want to study, create a Business Model Canvas for each company. Be thorough.

I once did a benchmark study for a company. In the study, I found the breadth of their offerings and compared all the marketing programs, terms and conditions of sale, price points, number of products in categories, and cataloging and marketing materials. I tried to compare everything there was to compare.

It did not take long in the study process before I realized there was an entire category of products where we underpriced items by about 30 percent compared to others in our niche. This was in a luxury industry; lower prices had no meaningful impact on sales volumes. The next price increase went straight to the bottom line with no reduction in revenues.

There were also conclusions to draw about product breadth of offering, distribution, and many other aspects of the way we competed.

Most companies do not take the time or effort to make this kind of study. I assure you, when they do; they often find the results to be enlightening.

A few quarters after completion of the study, we explored the acquisition of one of the competitors. In their minds, they had a product line they intended to compete with our best product line.

It was fascinating to learn this, as we were completely oblivious to their presence in this space in the market. Their sales results on that product line were miniscule in comparison to ours.

If you are doing a benchmark study, include web and social media practices as one of your points of investigation. How do your competitions' websites compare to yours? Is there more or less information, features, or the possibility for ecommerce?

Do your competitors write blogs? Do they send newsletters? Do they post to social media sites? How do your practices compare?

If you are creating a new website or launching a social media program, can you achieve competitive parity with your efforts? Do you gain a competitive advantage? According to a Salesforce Marketing survey, only 12 percent of marketers were strongly satisfied with their efforts. According to the Salesforce Fifth Edition State of Marketing Report, 2018, only 16 percent of marketers were, "completely satisfied with their overall marketing performance and the outcomes of their marketing investments."[1].

This level of concern should prompt you to do a bit of study to understand where you rank with the competition.

Study Your Target Customer Segment. The best way to understand your customer segment is to create a Value Proposition Canvas.

In many first-time attempts by B2B businesses, participants in this make the mistake of seeing certain companies as target segments. The reason this is a mistake because companies, per se, do not make purchasing decisions.

People in companies make these decisions. Similarly, when creating a canvas for a business to customer business, the assumption that everyone is a potential customer misses the mark.

Sometimes entrepreneurs focus on a target segment and miss the fact that other decision makers may be influential in the decision-making process. This is especially true when selling to enterprise companies. Sometimes several decision makers can influence the purchase. You need a solid value proposition for all of them.

In other cases, entrepreneurs are so invested and confident of their solution they can only envision customers who might buy what they do. This fallacy can lead to a situation where they end up targeting a market segment that is small, when a large segment might simply be adjacent to their thinking if they would make a pivot on their value proposition.

Another mistake is to draw conclusions too soon without observing the behaviors of a reasonable sample of target customers. Most start-up advisors suggest you need at least one hundred customers to validate your business model.

If you are in doubt whether you should view a group of people as a partner, resource, or customer, I recommend you move them to customer status.

Unless you reflect on it, you may miss the fact yours is a two-sided business model. Business models that connect a group of service providers with those who need the service are usually a two-sided model. To make a two-sided model work, you need a value proposition for both sides.

Another business model where you need to decide which segments are customers is two-stage distribution models.

A two-stage model is one where you sell to an intermediary like a wholesaler, value-added reseller, or distributor. In some cases, you can sell to the intermediary and to the next level of distribution including the end consumer.

Seeing "Companies who ..." as target segments
People make purchasing decisions, not companies

Ignoring key decision makers
People with the responsibility and spending authority make decisions

Not being honest about pain points
Rationalizing validation of your value proposition when the facts about customer needs are something else

Drawing conclusions too soon
Sample the behaviors of at least 100 customers to validate your conclusions

Viewing customers as partners or resources
Treat them as customers if a value proposition is important for them to work with you

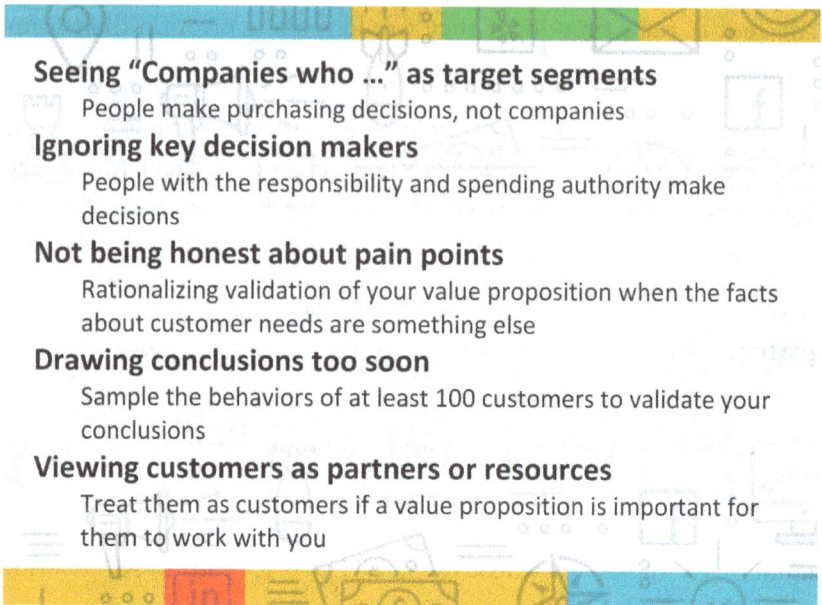

FIGURE 30. Common mistakes made when creating a value proposition canvas.

In the Context of Competition and Customer Need

The way you plan to compete should not be a decision made in a vacuum. If a competitor has a strong position for the way they compete, you might not want to confront them directly. If you conclude that the pain points for your target customer segment need a unique approach, then you must focus on ways to out-execute the competitor.

Many times, you will find there are opportunities no one has addressed. Changes in market size or technology may make an approach workable today when only a few years ago, you could not consider it. Some long-time competitors may be slow to change and remain stuck in the way they have always done things.

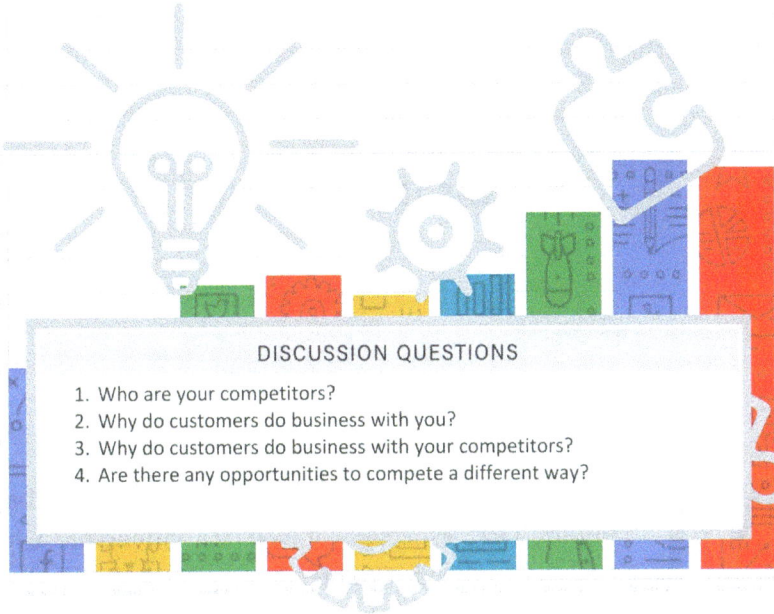

DISCUSSION QUESTIONS

1. Who are your competitors?
2. Why do customers do business with you?
3. Why do customers do business with your competitors?
4. Are there any opportunities to compete a different way?

22

MANAGING DETAILS

Managing your marketing and sales efforts can be a complex task, especially if you are vulnerable when details are missed. Chapter 2 suggested you devise a system for keeping score if you want to be playing the game.

One tool adopted by most enterprise businesses in small and medium size business is customer relationship management software (CRM).

This is a way to track the steps in your process for turning a lead into a customer and your later efforts to keep a customer.

I have seen this tool work well for some companies, but I have also seen struggles.

When the System is Unmanaged

In one case, a business invested in a customer relationship management application customized on a salesforce customer relationship management system platform. The company spent considerable funds to develop the customization. Users could create customer quotes without leaving the system and you could record every attribute about a customer.

It was not working for the company.

First, nobody was mandating use of the system. Salespeople were communicating with customers through email and phone calls, then not recording conversations and events in the system. Serving the customers needed a team of people and many relevant conversations and decisions, which users did not record.

The second issue had to do with operational maintenance by marketing. Marketing's responsibility included entering leads into the system. There were over one hundred leads, worth $3 million, not entered into the system. Nobody assigned salespeople to follow up on leads and opportunities expired due to inattention.

The third issue; the customer relationship management system did not digitally connect to the company's enterprise resource planning (ERP) system. When a lead became an order, all the detailed data had to be manually re-entered into the enterprise resource planning system.

Of course, once it was in the enterprise resource planning system, later order changes did not record in the customer relationship management system. Do you suppose prices were the same between the two systems? Nope, that was an issue too.

I used another custom salesforce customer relationship management system with another company. In this case, the cost per user was extremely high, and the company was reluctant to shift to a lower cost system because of the sunk cost of the customization.

Eventually, as customer relationship management systems became more functional and lower cost, the price differential was too much to continue to cling to the older, customized customer relationship management system.

In both experiences, the software customization enabled collection and filtering of more information about customers and potential customers. In both cases, this added effort by marketing and sales people to keep up the system. In other words, solving one pain point was at the expense of creating another pain point.

I must also note the user interfaces for both customized products were unbelievably bad. It was necessary to train, understand, and then practice where certain pieces of data were found. The user interface designs used approaches about the same as a small font, colorless spreadsheet.

Woulda, Coulda, Shoulda

I did not see the value in having the customer relationship management system customized in either case I mentioned. If you could spend the same money on a bi-directional data interface between the enterprise resource planning system and customer relationship management system, it would have been money better spent. Re-entering data adds no value to any process.

To mandate use of the system, all sales review meetings used reports from the system. Even then, it was a slog to get everyone to update his or her projects, especially if an order was lost. Especially consider the Lone Wolf sales profile. How anxious do you think they are to update the customer relationship management system?

It would have been good to know the why for lost orders, so we could have implemented remedies but the reasons noted by the salespeople seldom drilled down to root cause issues.

By policy, you were to enter new leads within forty-eight hours of receipt and assign them to salespeople within another forty-eight hours. This aspect of managing the system seemed to work well.

CONFIGURABLE
If a user can specify process steps and special data fields

CUSTOMIZABLE
If a special programmer, service, or expense is required

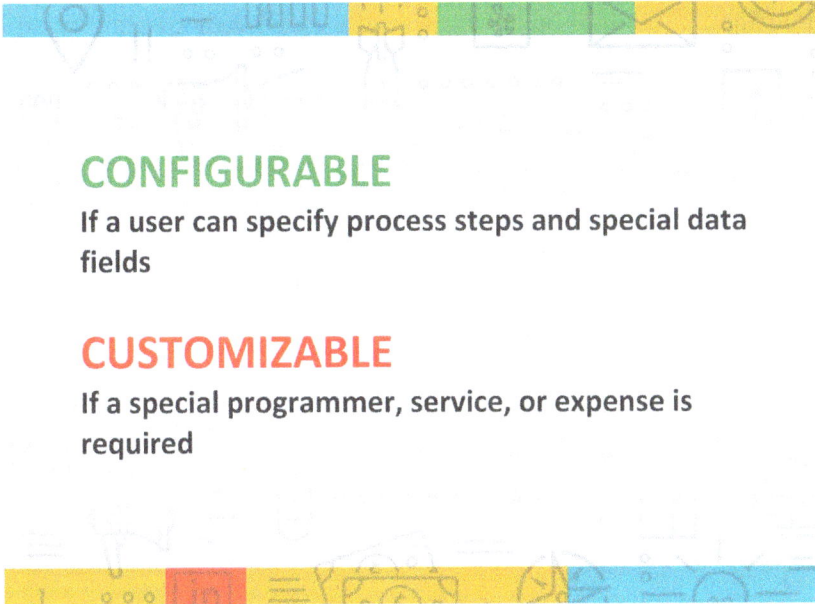

FIGURE 31. What is the difference between configuration and customization?

If you have a website where you generate leads, it would be a good practice to record these in a fashion that would allow you to enter them into your customer relationship management directly, or create a .csv file you can upload without manually re-entering information.

Selecting a Customer Relationship Management System

The customer relationship management customizations in my past were not particularly useful.

There are many new companies entering the industry. Most are SaaS companies with some extremely useful features and attractive pricing structures.

Since many of these companies are start-ups, guard against the possibility they may go out of business. Be sure it is easy for you to move data from one system to another. Most companies enable the creation of a .csv file for this purpose. In addition, most also allow information input to be done with a .csv file. You should specify *easy in, easy out* for any system you select. That way you can remedy the risk of obsolescence.

If you consider marketing and sales as a process, you should be able to configure the software to match the steps in your process using the exact terminology you otherwise use in your business. If you believe sales efforts are increasingly migrating towards

1) the Challenger sales model, and

2) where more complexity is involved, the configuration capabilities might be the single most important consideration in your customer relationship management system buying decision.

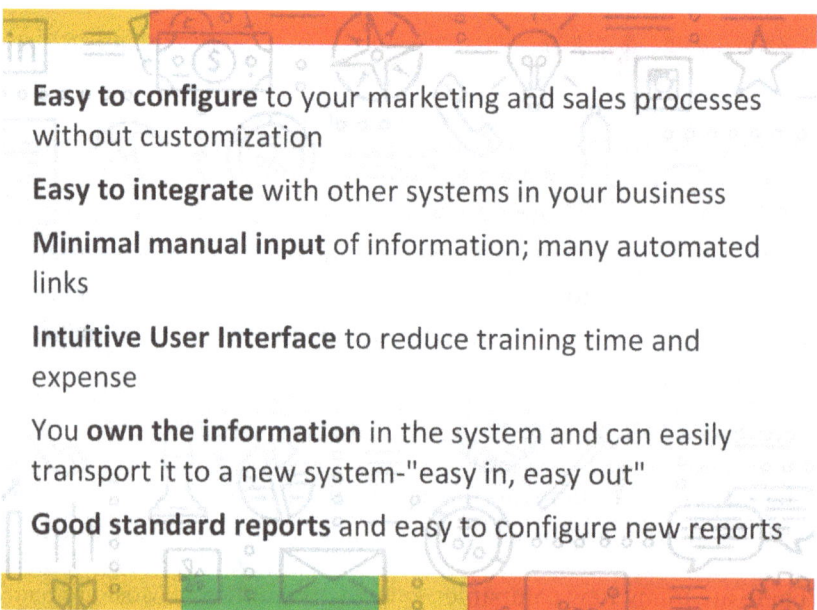

Easy to configure to your marketing and sales processes without customization

Easy to integrate with other systems in your business

Minimal manual input of information; many automated links

Intuitive User Interface to reduce training time and expense

You **own the information** in the system and can easily transport it to a new system-"easy in, easy out"

Good standard reports and easy to configure new reports

FIGURE 32. Six important considerations when selecting your CRM system.

Some companies are creating two-way data hubs that integrate systems. Said another way, if information in one system is changed and the same information is contained in other systems, the there is an automatic update in all systems. Before you select a customer relationship management system, you may consider the difficulty to add it to the hub.

I am a major fan of the data hub approach as it allows you to select best of class for each of your applications. The alternative is to use a cumbersome enterprise resource planning system that has customer relationship system included, but not necessarily the best products for individual applications.

There are also customer relationship management products that link web information about target customers to the customer relationship management system. Some search the web for information like Facebook and LinkedIn profiles so public information is part of your customer relationship management.

Maintaining a customer relationship management is not selling or marketing if the time to keep the system running is devoted to clerical tasks. Intuitive user interfaces, corresponding mobile apps, and automated links all reduce the non-value-added clerical tasks.

A good reporting system is also important. It may not be important to individual users, but managers and top executives should be able to quickly check the status and movement of the marketing and sales process. Graphs and charts are far more useful than rows and columns of numbers.

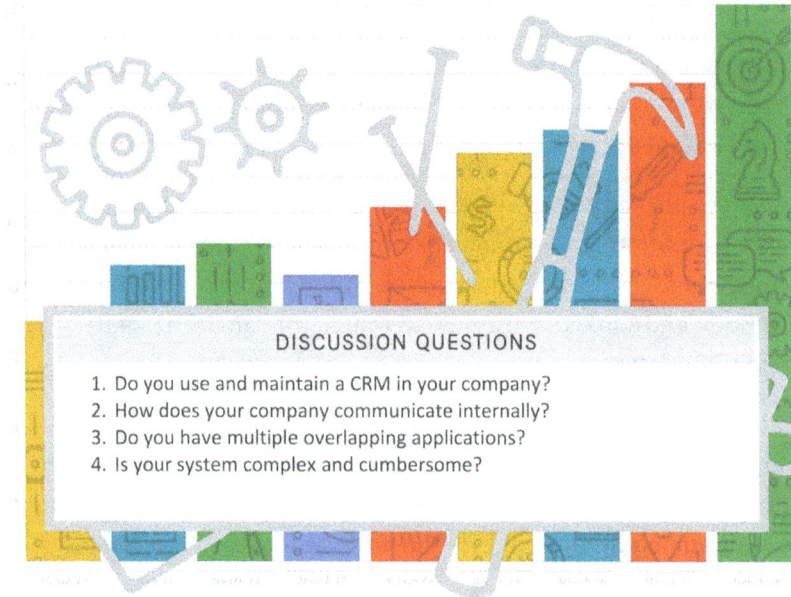

DISCUSSION QUESTIONS

1. Do you use and maintain a CRM in your company?
2. How does your company communicate internally?
3. Do you have multiple overlapping applications?
4. Is your system complex and cumbersome?

23

SEVEN WASTES IN MARKETING AND SALES

L ean thinking (a.k.a. the Toyota Production System) identifies seven categories of waste found in any process. The lean start-up movement urges you to conduct experiments with your business model before you commit resources to building your products. Strategyzer[1] encourages you to create a Business Model Canvas[2] and a Value Proposition Canvas[3] so you can easily envision your strategic planning.

Consider and evaluate your marketing and sales processes in the context of these effective management tools.

In lean thinking, one role of the top executive leader is to bring leadership to the efforts to find and end wastes in processes. As a CEO, founder, or owner, if you are working in the business rather than on the business, you are wasting time in your role. Someone in your business should be improving processes, you.

Seven Sins

Some types of waste are blatantly obvious. Other forms of waste may be subtler.

Overproduction

Producing ahead of what is needed by the next step in the process such as too many social media posts, too many leads, more orders than capacity.

Waiting

Staff standing idle as batch order processes cycle, equipment fails, or needed information is missing.

Conveyance

Moving leads, quotes, or orders unnecessarily, from one processing step to another processing step when the second step instead could be immediate.

Processing

Performing unnecessary or incorrect processing, typically from bad information.

Inventory

Having more than the minimum items necessary for a controlled pull system such as unrecorded leads, unassigned leads, unprocessed quote requests.

Motion

Making movements that are unnecessary, such as looking for emails, quotes, and specifications.

Correction

Inspection, rework, and scrap to cover bad order entry, poor specifications, or sending a wrong item or service staff member.

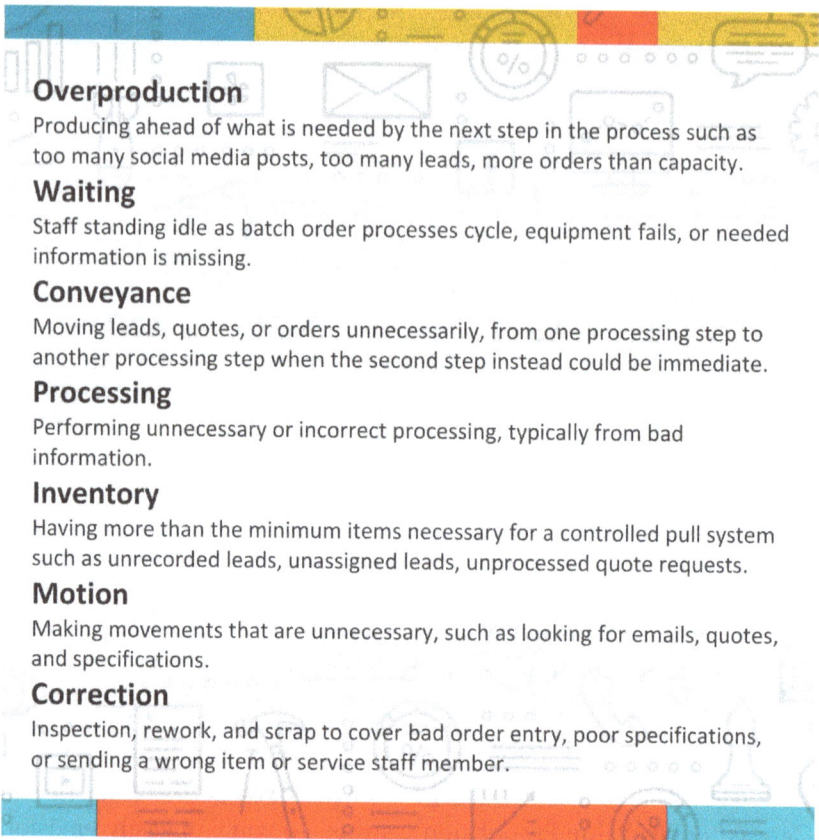

FIGURE 33. Wastes that could be in your sales and marketing process.

Figure 33 summarizes the seven categories of waste typically as taught by the gurus in lean thinking, with examples of wastes that might be in your marketing and sales processes.

Overproduction occurs when you spend time and/or money on something that is more than earlier or subsequent needs in your process flow. If you generate more leads than can be followed up by your sales team, what is the value of the surplus leads? If your sales team generates more orders than your operations can produce, or said another way ... late shipments, what is the value to your business?

Some businesses, experienced in lean thinking, set sales and production targets first in their operational planning cycles. The marketing and sales team, as well as the operations team, then organize themselves to meet the target, not more, not less.

Can this apply to a SaaS company? I would argue yes. If your systems have inadequate computing ability, you may lose customers because of slow response times. If you invest in too much computing ability, you are paying for something you did not need.

In addition, there is the ability of your customer service operations, your accounting processes, and your hiring and training processes to consider. You are making the best uses of your resources if all is in balance.

When you take anything in your business to excess, you create waste.

I was once in a situation where the chairman of our company was relentlessly making acquisitions. When I raised the issue about the prudence of ignoring post-close integration, he told me "... you guys in operations are just going to have to keep up. As long as I can raise money, I'm going to keep buying."

It was so chaotic that at one time I had over thirty issues noted on a single piece of paper; each with more than a $1 million impact and simply no one who could answer any question I had. Unbelievably, no one assigned a manager to one acquired facility. The team at that location sensed they had no go-forward role and gave themselves lucrative severance agreements.

It was not long after this that the whole acquisition scheme collapsed under its own weight. The company spent hundreds of millions of dollars on a process that was not in balance.

Waiting occurs when there is an interruption in a process. Suppose you are configuring and entering an order from a customer into your business system, for example. If needed information is missing, you are waiting. One way to understand waiting is to consider the minutes or hours it takes an order to pass through your system. Then compare that to the elapsed time. For most companies, the difference is large. Understanding the reasons for the difference can lead you to solutions that reduce the waiting. When you work to cut the delays in the process, it is highly likely you will also realize meaningful cost benefits.

Conveyance refers to movement. Let us suppose you have a business with multiple physical locations. If you generate applications or requests for quote or other forms of paperwork or materials sent to a central location, the waste you see is the movement. Even the travel inside of a building adds no value and is waste.

Some companies create functional departments. This means an item, whether it is a physical item or paperwork must travel from each physical department to the next.

The alternative is to arrange processing steps physically next to each other. If you do this, it is easy to see where bottlenecks are in the system.

Processing waste occurs when you make scrap. Incorrect information such as incorrect quantities on a quote creates a scrap quote. Missing information also creates waste. Other examples include bad addresses, email lists without updates, spelling errors in marketing collateral materials, and wrong shipping addresses.

Inventory is the waste I most disdain. You should always have a mental picture of inventory as a stack of dollar bills. When something is stuck in an inventory, it seems only bad things can happen. Items can be lost, damaged, and become obsolete.

When inventories are large, you are compelled to count them. For physical goods, you must value them and show them as assets on your balance sheet. This adds no value other than satisfying your accountant.

Inventories do not have to be just physical items. Anywhere in a process where there is a queue; like a stack of leads, uncompleted quotes, or orders waiting to be processed, you have inventory.

Motion waste is people making unnecessary movements. Looking for parts, documents, or even searching online for a file is waste. If you observe carefully, you can find one or more people in your company who are searching for something at any given moment.

Correction waste has to do with inspecting, reworking, and scrapping earlier work. Doing it over is far costlier than doing something right the first time. In your marketing and sales processes, think about the edits that go into the creation of a newsletter, blog post, or social media post. It could also be a bad quote or proposal, or the costs when you send the wrong item or assign the wrong staff member.

I know of a company that had millions of combinations and permutations of their product lines. At the beginning of their order entry process, they were manually creating specifications for each order.

Until a customer received their product, there was no way to know if it was a correctly specified order. They had a major profit issue, as there was no way to dispose of the defective product already produced.

Finally, a solution at the beginning of the process, a configurator, automated the specification process and reduced the bad order entry errors.

If You Can See Waste, You Can Eliminate It

Seeing waste is a skill you can develop. Many companies fall into a trap where they do the same things repeatedly, even though waste is right under their nose.

I have seen multiple instances where staff creates reports with metrics, but nobody bothers to read and interpret the reports. It was as if the creation of the report was the goal. No one realized the real value to a report is to see issues.

You cannot end waste if you cannot see it. So, seeing it is your first step. However, the second step might be just as important.

This is where you get to be creative. Ask yourself or your team to see if there are ways to end the waste. Can you change the process? Do you need a tool? Does there need to be a software update? What is the best way to cut waste?

FIGURE 34. *If you do not look, you cannot see waste.*

Asking people to try to do better the next time is not an effective way to end waste. Look for sustainable changes you can make to the process rather than relying on human diligence to ensure your success.

Do not Be Dismissive

For many companies, a 10 percent net profit is a satisfactory performance. If you look at your marketing and sales expenses as a percent of net sales, you will see them as 20 percent, give or take a few points.

If you can be serious about cutting waste in your process for your 10 percent-profit company, for example, could you reduce your marketing and sales expenses by 2 percent? If you could do this, you might increase your profits by 20 percent.

For companies where valuation is primarily determined by cash flow, the same math applies. A 2 percent increase in cash flow could be a 20 percent increase in valuation.

Ending waste is not a trivial task.

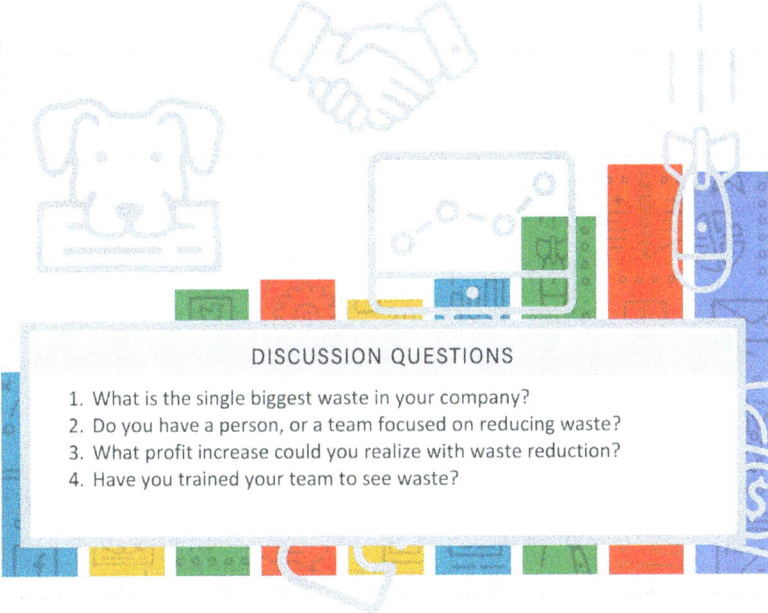

DISCUSSION QUESTIONS

1. What is the single biggest waste in your company?
2. Do you have a person, or a team focused on reducing waste?
3. What profit increase could you realize with waste reduction?
4. Have you trained your team to see waste?

24

WHAT COULD POSSIBLY GO WRONG?

There is an important waste I did not address in chapter 21, I have reviewed dozens of financial statements in my career and there is a waste which seems like it is nonrecurring, but I often find it when I perform due diligence.

It is the cost of dealing with a dispute.

I find it almost humorous when business brokers and investment bankers refer to these as nonrecurring expenses. If you look at the details of any specific case, they are correct. The exact dispute seldom occurs twice. The brokers and investment bankers frame this as an add-back, an expense that should be ignored when calculating the cash flow and valuation of a company.

I know of few businesses that run for more than a few years that do not have a dispute to resolve. What is recurring is the presence of a dispute, not the nature of the dispute. My business sensibilities are offended when told to ignore legal costs completely when calculating cash flow. There are always legal expenses. In addition, they all reduce cash flow, which is why the broker or investment banker wants you to look the other way.

These disputes always rise to the level of the top executive's office as few people in your organization will be willing to manage these kinds of issues unless they have experience, your trust, and authority to act.

This may be an extreme example but in 2017, Uber reported it was dealing with 433 separate lawsuits. In that company, dealing with lawsuits has become a business process itself[1].

I have seen businesses who try to save money by skirting the law. I have seen managers, for example, who operate with no agreements, knowingly avoid necessary permits, fail to pay owed commissions, fail to pay required overtime, mis-classify employees, improperly dispose of hazardous wastes, deny valid customer warranty claims, and ignore sexual harassment issues (a seemingly high correlation to salespeople).

Avoiding preventative legal defenses might be a way to maximize your legal costs.

Your marketing and sales process is not immune to disputes. There are measures you can take to prevent or limit the impact of a dispute. While these have a cost to implement, they are far less costly than out-of-control lawsuits. The first step you should take is to recognize and put a placeholder in your budget for your legal defenses.

Find an Attorney You Trust

The next step in building your defenses for legal issues is to find an appropriately qualified attorney to support you in managing legal issues.

There are two types of attorneys: transactional and litigation. A transactional attorney is what you need first to help you with oversight. They will be a generalist whose focus spans a wide range of business issues. The term most used for this by many businesses is general counsel.

Transactional lawyers typically prepare contracts, file applications (i.e. trademark and patent filings) with courts and government agencies, and sometimes negotiate terms between companies. They are the ones that strategize a company's moves to keep that business out of trouble such as putting them in a stronger position to discourage lawsuits.

If you are a small business or a start-up, there are transactional attorneys who provide this kind of support on a part-time basis. You can engage them for an hourly fee. I also know attorneys who work for a modest, affordable monthly retainer. You can call them any time for any reason.

Your general counsel can usually help you with the everyday and simplest issues. When there is a dispute that needs specialized knowledge, they can help you with a referral to the other type of attorney, the litigation attorney.

Litigation attorneys are usually the ones you go to when all your dispute resolution efforts fail. Litigation attorneys look for the best resolution for their clients. The best resolution may be a negotiated settlement, a mediation hearing, a trial, or some other choice. Because the options are not always clear or easy to reach, once you enter the realm of litigation the costs to the business/client can skyrocket.

When you are involved in managing this, I suggest you reflect on how you select litigation counsel. The lowest cost attorney may result in the highest cost dispute if they are not sufficiently experienced or skilled.

In my past, I hired attorneys who were fourth degree connections with a high hourly cost. Doing deep, intense networking and diligence on your choice may be the best way to win or limit the cost of a dispute. I cannot speak for others, but my experience suggests this is a key decision. In my career, I consider myself almost undefeated when I use this tactic. This may be another counter-intuitive concept but the actions you take at the beginning of a dispute may be the key to limiting your exposure.

In the US, a dispute that settles in a courtroom costs a minimum of $250,000 for each side of the dispute. An attorney, skilled at settling out of court, is a way to limit your expenses.

If the flow of legal issues becomes more intense, you may employ a general counsel on your team. This gives you a way to deal with the volume and someone who knows how to manage the outsourced support.

If your company is bigger yet, you may create a legal department that handles some issues internally and outsources others.

Prevention and Limitation

Your approach should include a proper array of necessary documents and agreements. These could include employee agreements with commission structures, independent contractor agreements, non-disclosure agreements, terms and conditions of sale or terms of service agreements, general release agreements, employee termination agreements, intellectual property agreements, order acknowledgements, warranties, returns policies, consignment agreements, and patents and trademarks.

In addition, there are policies, programs, and other promises you make to customers, distributors, and employees. While these may not be legal agreements in the strictest sense, have your counsel review these also to ensure they conform to all applicable laws. Be sure to communicate in a way that limits exposure.

This is not a comprehensive list. You should also recognize much of the expense for creating your legal defense is a one-time, up-front cost.

All of these are ways you can limit your legal expenses. Legal disputes are waste. They add no value to your company.

Know that you need to manage legal expenses
  Find and engage general counsel support
  Aim to limit your costs
Anticipate and cover all the contingencies
  Put policies into effect before an event
  Communicate your policies, preferably on your website
Manage legal matters as you would operations
  Involve your counsel in routine decisions
  Manage your attorney
  Manage your cases
Try to remain objective and dispassionate
  Settling concerns or disputes is easier if you act sooner rather than later
  Usually, the best (or least bad) outcomes occur when neither side is completely satisfied

FIGURE 35. Minimizing waste on legal expenses depends on your approach.

Put Your Defenses Where They Can Be Seen

If you understand the need to create your legal defenses, also understand the need to communicate them. Your website is a particularly good place as everyone who interacts with your business visits your site.

When you are specifying the design of your website, consider where to place your legal documents and policies. Some you want the public to see. Others may involve an authorization and login system. If certain documents are specific to certain customer segments or employees, consider having multiple secure pages in your design.

Do not let this be an afterthought to your website design specifications. You might opt for a standard template then later discover you have legal matters to consider better handled with a more custom approach.

Try to present your position in the most positive and easily understood way when relating your business policies. Some attorneys draft certain documents in all capital letters. In today's online business world, this is yelling. I have a tough time understanding why this is necessary. Challenge them to make your communication thorough and friendly.

You might also try to design summaries or highlights to certain policies as way to be friendlier in your approach. However, be sure your legal counsel agrees.

Another consideration is document control. When you have several documents, inevitably there are some that you revise, change, or drop and replace.

It is a good practice to choose a place to keep the master copy. Consider all others as copies of the master. This can be an arbitrary decision.

If you use your website as the home of the master copy, then you can be sure the document that faces your customers and your company is the most-current, fully approved master copy. The other choice is to risk someone is using the wrong document.

Manage a Case and Manage Your Attorney

While you should strive to put as many defensive measures in place as possible, you will still have disputes that arise.

My first advice to you is to understand and treat an issue as you would stages of grief. At first, you will experience denial; *this cannot be happening*, and, *why does it have to happen?*

Next, you will be angry. Do not take any action when you are angry.

You might be angry with a customer, or an employee, or your attorney. You might attack convenient, though innocent targets.

Then you will try to bargain. *if only our policy included ... If only we had acted sooner ... If only I handled that myself ...*

Then you could become depressed. You might wake in the middle of the night bothered by the issue. You may withdraw and experience sadness and regret.

At the next stage, you finally reach acceptance and are ready to move on. When you can finally become dispassionate about an issue, you are in the best place to resolve disputes and limit your expenses.

Some leaders never get to this point in the process.

One of the most challenging cases I managed in my career was an intellectual property dispute. My involvement began in the middle of the case when I joined the company.

We had a product line sourced through a decades-long-time supplier who had the products produced in Asia. The company where I worked wanted to create another version of the product line. The supplier balked. The reason, which I later came to understand, was there was not enough volume to manage an Asian supply chain easily and extending the product line would add management complexity.

Rather than resolve this issue, my company decided to source the product with a second supplier.

The first supplier claimed my company had wrongfully used their intellectual property and produced designs too like the originals. When I examined this assertion, I found plenty of evidence to suggest this was not true. Likely, we could prevail if ever the issue could focus on the facts.

The first supplier filed suit in US Federal Court.

My boss, who was managing the case before my involvement, hired a law firm for defense whose specialty was to compel insurance companies who issued general liability policies to defend intellectual property disputes.

When I came into the case, I discovered my boss consumed emotionally and doing nothing to manage the attorneys nor working towards a resolution. The attorneys were managing themselves and the ever-mounting legal costs were reaching a level equal to a year's worth of gross margin on the product line.

The plaintiff, equally emotionally charged as my boss, irrationally pursued the case.

At the same time, our attorneys had not compelled our insurance company to defend and I was still getting legal bills.

To change the course of this case, I finally had to demand our attorneys STOP WORKING (yes, I yelled) until the principal of the law firm could explain what plausible course of action was to be taken to resolve the case.

The result was a meeting with the federal judge in the case, the plaintiff, the plaintiff's attorney, our attorney, and me. Our attorney explained his aim to everyone. The judge agreed, and our attorney, the plaintiff's attorney, and the judge colluded on restating the plaintiff's claims in the case to compel the insurance company to become a defendant.

It worked and in the next meeting, all the same parties were present plus a representative from the insurance company.

We reached a settlement, but I had to be a bit creative. The plaintiff wanted a lump sum payment plus a royalty going forward. I countered with a reduced, insurance-feasible lump sum payment but a much higher royalty.

The plaintiff agreed, and the insurance company paid the lump sum. The case settled.

Finally, no one won this case.

My company never bought anything from the plaintiff again. We dropped the product line, so no royalties were ever paid. Of course, I knew this would be our way forward when I put together the counter offer that prompted the settlement.

Our law firm earned scorn rather than an endorsement from us. The insurance company wrote a big check. The plaintiff lost a customer. My company lost a product line and a revenue stream.

Moreover, I wasted a lot of my time on a non-value-added issue.

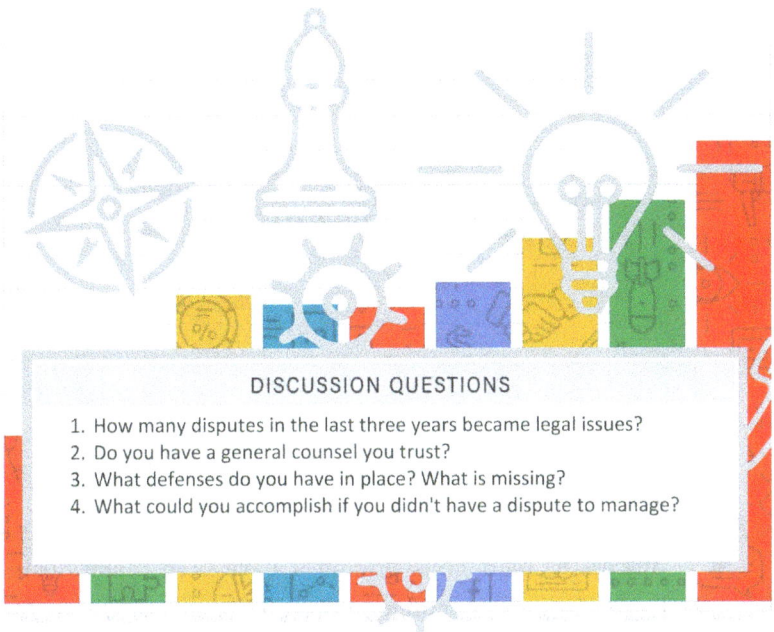

DISCUSSION QUESTIONS

1. How many disputes in the last three years became legal issues?
2. Do you have a general counsel you trust?
3. What defenses do you have in place? What is missing?
4. What could you accomplish if you didn't have a dispute to manage?

25

THE RIGHT PRICE

A nother important aspect of your marketing and sales process to manage is pricing. I have seen many business leaders who do not adequately appreciate managing prices in their businesses.

Why is Pricing Important?

Healthy businesses typically earn profits equal to 10 percent of their revenues before taxes. All things being equal a 3 percent price increase can increase profit dollars for such a business by 30 percent.

If cost increases in a business amount to 3 percent of revenues and the company does not increase prices, the impact would be to reduce profits by 30 percent.

It is important for you as a CEO to maintain prices in a way that, at the very least, sustains your margins, covers your expenses and maintains your profit model.

One piece of advice I once received about the mentality of budgeting; the proper way to create a budget was to determine profits first, then add expected expenses, add the cost of goods sold, and then price products and services according to the profit model you created.

At first, I wrongly thought this advice to be too obvious. I have encountered other approaches. Some managers believe lowering prices could be a way to build market share. Others fear the loss of customers if they raise prices.

Some business owners manage their pricing, so it provides them a reasonable salary. If they are satisfied with the money they take out of the business to support their personal lifestyle, then they are satisfied with their pricing strategy.

The biggest fallacy in this thinking becomes painfully obvious when they decide to exit the business.

When selling a business, a rational buyer will determine the cash flow generated by the business.

In the world of finance, this is also known as EBITDA, or earnings before interest taxes, depreciation, and amortization.

Few people can buy a business with their own wealth. Financing is needed for most business sales. Lenders who make these loans want to know how they will get their loans repaid so they look at the cash flow from the business, adjusted for a normal salary to an owner.

If that adjustment calculation suggests there is no excess cash available to repay a loan, a buyer cannot secure financing. Moreover, a seller will not be able to sell their business.

By most estimates, at least 80 percent of all businesses in the US that come for sale never sell.

There are hundreds of thousands of businesses like this in the US. Many owners are dealing with the challenges of managing a business for a return that is nothing more than a salary.

A few years ago, I visited with a retail property owner with a similar perspective. According to him, there are many business owners where the net profits are less than the owners could make elsewhere if they merely earned the minimum wage.

Managing Pricing

One best practice when managing your prices is to assess your position annually. This cadence for review is usually enough. In the 1970s, high inflation was so pervasive many businesses made adjustments every six months. This business climate may return.

If you adjust prices less often, you could unnecessarily shock your customers with too large an increase. If you can live with increases in a range of 2 to 5 percent, most customers will take the increase in stride and make no fuss.

While the overall economy might not be currently experiencing inflation, there are specific industries and locales where there are issues.

I know of a fast-growing service business where it is becoming difficult to recruit service providers. The correct approach for this situation is to pay more and charge more.

Another best practice to avoid a pricing fuss is to give adequate notice about the timing of your increase. Establish a date for the increase and announce that all orders received before the announced date will price at the old price.

Some businesses that experience seasonal fluctuations in their demand will time their price increases to occur during the low demand part of the year. To the extent customers can control the timing of their purchases, the price increase deadline shifts demand into a period that otherwise might be a slowdown.

How much notice should you give customers? I suggest between sixty and ninety days. If you are a B2B business, this is especially important as this allows enough time for your customers to adjust their pricing for their customers.

If you are a B2C business, the amount and timing of a price increase may not be as critical. I know one company that adjusts prices continually with changes on a few items every month.

With businesses where the target customer is a one-time or short term, you can adopt a practice where you increase prices for new customers, and let old prices go away through attrition.

Some businesses still publish an elaborate, attractive, printed price list akin to collateral marketing materials. This can become a barrier to increasing prices if every change requires an expense like a capital expenditure. A best practice is to use a very modest form for communicating prices. Marketing collateral should be a separate thought.

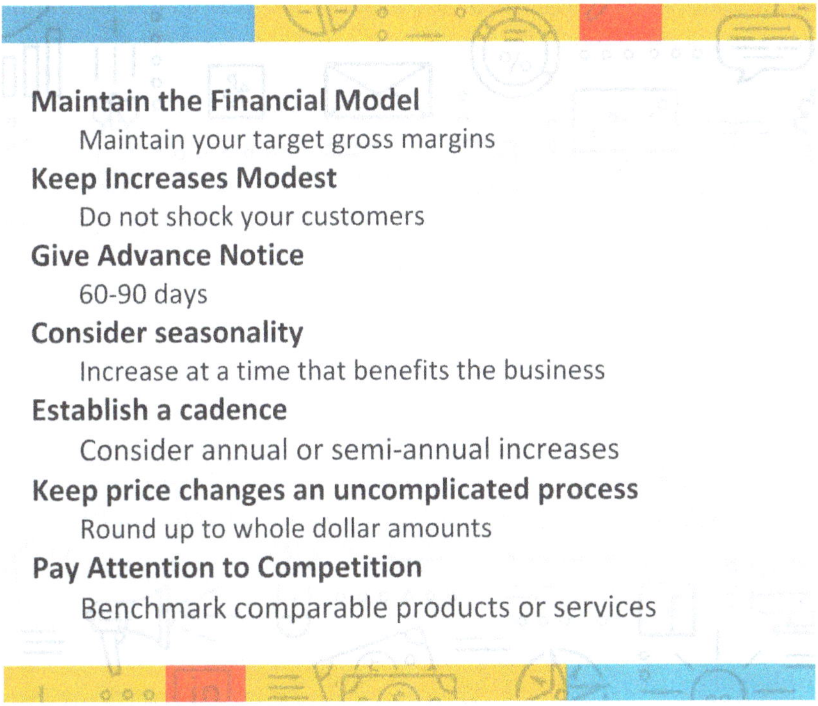

Maintain the Financial Model
Maintain your target gross margins
Keep Increases Modest
Do not shock your customers
Give Advance Notice
60-90 days
Consider seasonality
Increase at a time that benefits the business
Establish a cadence
Consider annual or semi-annual increases
Keep price changes an uncomplicated process
Round up to whole dollar amounts
Pay Attention to Competition
Benchmark comparable products or services

FIGURE 36. Simple considerations for managing pricing.

Complex Pricing

As more businesses adopt mass customization as a strategy for serving their customers, the pricing process becomes complex.

One approach to this problem is to manually conduct reviews, mandate approvals, and perform audits as part of your process.

A better way is to ask your IT people to put a configurator at the beginning of your process. With a configurator, the system knows all the options and associated prices. By using a series of pull-down menus, determining prices is simply a matter of detailing the specifications.

I know of one situation where a company had millions of combinations and permutations on their product line. Before finding mistakes, the company entered, manufactured, and shipped customer orders. This quality issue was painful to the business because there was no straightforward way to salvage the miss-specified product.

When they added a configurator to their business system, not only was the quoting process simpler, the accuracy of specification problem went away.

Pricing Tactics

There are a few other approaches to pricing to consider.

One is the hub and spoke approach. If you have an item in your product line or service offering that is a commodity and a large part of your revenue stream, you can make it the price leader. It would typically have lower margins (the hub) and the price for other items (the spokes) would have higher margins.

This works if you are confident customers will routinely buy the spokes when they buy the hub. The volume-weighted margin would be the critical metric.

There is also the good-better-best approach, three combinations of features and benefits at three price points. The good price point is low enough to attract attention but is usually associated with a minimum product or service.

The better price point is the one where you expect or intend to realize most of your sales. Margins for the better price point should be at your desired overall financial model targets.

The purpose of the best price point is to make the better price point look like a particularly good deal. The best product or service you have should be priced with high margins and have every feature including the kitchen sink.

When I worked in product development, we sometimes used another tactic that we called bracketing.

With this tactic, we would first study the price points and feature/benefits of the competition. Then we would conceive a product at a slightly lower price than the competition's better product and another more featured product at a price above the competition's better product.

The notion was to squeeze the competitor. If they moved their price point down, they would lose margin. If they added features, they would add to their cost structure.

One of the most successful launches I know involved the identification of a successful competitive product, then substituting for one costly feature. It was, "just as good as ...," except for one feature and it was one-third less price.

Should you raise the price on every item when you execute a price increase? No. There can be exceptions.

There was one product line when I was managing product engineering where the pricing, according to the research from our marketing department, was about 100 percent of the industry price. In other words, we had no price advantage.

The product line had decent margins, but it was a commodity product with no meaningful value proposition. Sales of the product line languished and there was no discernable revenue growth for several years. We had a small market share so there was plenty of upside potential for us.

We decided to shock the market a separate way. We lowered the price by 20 percent.

We at once had a value proposition and sales took off. Within two years, volume doubled on the product line. The price difference was enough to overcome the switching cost issue with customers.

What happened with the margins? The volume increase was so large it led to efficiencies in manufacturing and opened opportunities for capital investment and automation.

Two years after the price decrease, margins were the same.

Foolishly, a few years later, another manager tried the same strategy on another product line. He did not consider he was starting with a line that had a high market share.

This move failed miserably. There was no upside potential and a price decrease did nothing to increase demand for the line.

Who Should Determine Prices?

Use price changes recommended by your marketing department as your first choice. They should have knowledge about the competition and do the necessary research. Likely, there will be disagreements and it would be good for you to understand the details of these.

What is the necessary research? You should be able to reference a price list from every competitor. You should have any marketing collateral materials you can gather from the competition, so you can assess the features and benefits of competitive products and services.

Some companies' marketing departments create a marketing library where this content is stored. A handy way to do this would be files that are stored in the cloud.

If you create a library, support it and keep it current. Most companies put a date on their price lists. When you see a price list over six months old, you should make allowances when you do comparisons.

The other thing to consider about dates is to map them onto a calendar. Is your price increase the first or last to be implemented? Are you following or leading?

One big mistake made by many entrepreneurs is to determine prices from a cost. In other words, they determine their cost, and then add 30 to 40 percent to arrive at a price. This method completely ignores competition.

The pricing mistakes could go in either direction if you begin with your cost. If a competitor has a more efficient process, does that figure into your calculus? You could be overpriced. If you have better sources for materials, you might have an advantage. You could be underpriced.

The marketplace determines prices, not your costs.

A choice you should not make is to delegate the project to someone from your sales department. Salespeople, especially commissioned salespeople, usually do not perfectly align with your profit optimization motives. You compensate them for top line growth, not bottom-line growth.

What is the risk if you assign the price increase task to a salesperson? Read on.

How to do Pricing the Wrong Way

Initially, I was at a distance from this project. Several issues with the business consumed my bandwidth.

My boss assigned the project to the vice president of sales. The general direction given was to increase prices by 5 percent with some products a bit more, some less. It had been eighteen months since the earlier increase; there was an urgency to adjust.

A few months later, I was becoming concerned as I expected to see the price increase telegraph through our financial statements. We should have been seeing higher margins.

Nothing was changing.

A month or two later there was still no noticeable effect. Now I was in the audit mode trying to understand what happened, to explain the lack of a monetary impact.

This was not an easy task as we had a very unfriendly business system, so I had to resort to a study using an Excel spreadsheet. There were several hundred items to consider.

My spreadsheet included the item, old price, new price, and quantities sold since the announced date of the price increase. Then I did calculations.

What I discovered was there were bigger price increases on lower volume items and little or no increases on the high-volume items. While prices increased on 90 percent of the items, they only increased on 20 percent of the sales volume.

Our intended 5 percent price increase was really a 1 percent increase. We left 4 percent on the table and it was too late to react. Unless we wanted to shock our customers, there was no way to recover immediately. It would take several years to creep the prices upward to compensate.

DISCUSSION QUESTIONS

1. Do you have a process for adjusting your prices?
2. How does your pricing compare to the competition?
3. Are you satisfied with your margins and net profits?
4. Who recommends price changes in your company?

26

GREASE THE SQUEAKY WHEEL

How do you keep from getting pulled into everyday issues in your marketing and sales process? If your personality is detail oriented, it is easy to get yourself involved in minutiae. Every time you do this, however, it comes at the expense of spending your time on something strategic. Is using the CEO's, owner's, or founder's time to manage details the wrong way to be effective? Is it another waste to add to the list in chapter 22?

Of course, it is.

You have only x amount of personal bandwidth in your day, and many other processes to manage. How can you be sure everything is running smoothly without becoming personally involved? What is the antidote?

Empowerment

The most important way to keep things running smoothly is to empower people to act independently.

The best experience I had was in one case where the corporate CEO put his thoughts in writing in the form of an authority document. It outlined what I could spend on my own as well as when I needed one or more signatures from managers above me. There was also clarity about hiring and firing practices included in the document.

Spending authority was a broad term. Included were obvious expenditures for things like equipment purchases and other fixed assets. The term also meant consulting and services agreements, acquisitions, write-offs, leases, and asset disposals.

Nothing about this experience was particularly a surprise, except for one thing. My personal spending authority was $500,000.

I was early in my general management career and could not imagine ever spending that amount without consulting someone to discuss the decision. I think the CEO knew that but wanted to make a statement about trust. This was my biggest take-away from the experience.

Several years later, I executed the concept another way. Rather than an authority document, I used the term empowerment document and extended it to everyone in the company. I said that anyone in even the lowest position could spend $100 without asking permission.

In practice, few people spent any money. More important was the knowledge that they could if they needed something to aid them to do their job.

Many CEOs have authority well past $500,000. I know of one case where a CEO can spend $25 million without asking permission of his board. I cannot say this with certainty, but I doubt he acts unilaterally in practice.

The creation of a document prompts a discussion around the expectations for independent action and trust. This may be the most important aspect.

In managing your marketing and sales process, your empowerment document should also consider some other issues. Who has the responsibility and authority to approve marketing materials or blog posts or social media content?

What are the authority levels for making quotes, setting prices, or giving discounts? Who has the responsibility and authority to approve refunds to customers?

Who has the responsibility and authority to assign leads to salespeople? On the other hand, who can take them away?

There are, of course, limits to your delegation. You should carefully consider when you want involvement in an operational decision. Does your involvement depend on the size or scale of an issue? Are there certain customers that should be exceptions?

If your empowerment document is too limiting, you will find yourself spending more time on operational issues than you might wish. If you find yourself unwilling to trust a subordinate, you might want to reflect on their fit for the job.

Another pitfall occurs when you find yourself drawn into an issue, then repeatedly agreeing with the proposed solution. This might be a sign subordinates are insecure about themselves and they delegate upward, also known as subordinate-imposed time.

If you want to do a deeper dive on this, there is an almost-timeless article from the Harvard Business Review. One of the two all-time best-selling reprints is Management Time: Who's Got the Monkey[1], published originally in 1974.

The Water Beetle

I also like another concept that comes from lean thinking. Name someone to be the water beetle.

A water beetle is a special person in your organization. The water beetle completely understands everything you are trying to carry out in your process. This highly skilled person could step into any job as necessary.

Their sole job is to keep everyone else in the organization busy in their jobs.

If you could watch your business from above, you would see this person move about your company at random to other people, like a ... water beetle. They see what is happening and react to anything that might result in a delay or bottleneck in your process. In other words, they are on duty continuously to deal with the little issues you and your managers might otherwise have to address.

Not every company calls this position a water beetle. I know some who refer to it as quarterback. In other words, most of the time someone else calls the plays and the quarterback as a member of the team leads execution. In addition, like a quarterback in football, they have the authority to change the play if they know it is not going to work.

Whenever you have a process, there are inevitably events that interrupt the process. Quality issues, missing materials, or absentees are reasons that stop production. Someone needs to deal with these issues as they occur.

It should not be you or your managers.

A HIGH-VALUE TEAM MEMBER

Observes and reacts to process slowdowns

Supplements efforts of others who slow the process

Ensures all necessary tools and supplies are available

On-boards and mentors inexperienced staff members

Problem solves challenges

Knows how to organize the team to meet deadlines

Reviews and approves marketing content

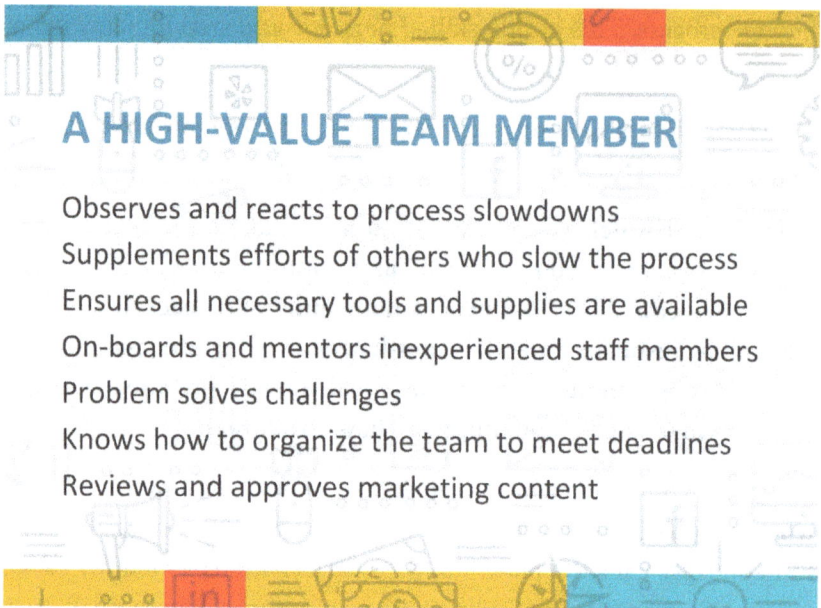

FIGURE 37. What does the water beetle do? Here are some suggestions.

Who is a Fit for This Role?

The first important qualification is end-to-end knowledge of your process. The person is someone with at least a few years seniority as it takes time to learn and experience the challenges in your process. They are detail oriented and respected by others in the organization, not only for what they know about the specifics of your process but also for their good judgment and commitment to results.

The people who fit best for this role have a steadying personality and calming influence. They are not a manager. In fact, they have no interest in managing others. They simply want to see the gears turning in the business. Likely, you see them as one of the best employees you have. They are reliable and trustworthy. They work well with their peers and the organization respects them.

If you want to know what's going on, this is the person who can explain the situation.

In many companies, there are awards for employee of the year. If you have a program like this in your company, you know you want to select someone who will be an example to others. These are good candidates to consider for your water beetle (or quarterback) position.

Pay them just a bit less than their direct manager but more than you pay their peers. If you cannot see your way to this, your candidate is not qualified or ready for the job.

DISCUSSION QUESTIONS

1. Are you spending too much time on operations and not enough time on strategy?
2. Who are your most skilled and trusted subordinates?
3. What would happen if you gave more authority to key people?
4. Can you take a vacation and not be bothered?

27

THE PROCESS FOR MANAGING THE PROCESS

Moore's Law[1] has impacted me most of my career. The university I attended had entire building devoted to an IBM Model 360. In my college-days co-op engineering experience, my company had an IBM Model 370.

I took courses for Fortran Programming, Cobol programming, Simulation using GPSS, and dynamic simulation. Shortly after graduating, I taught myself basic query language (BQL) that was like sorting and filtering in spreadsheets but done on a mainframe computer. The user interface with the computer was paper punch cards.

Grades in the college courses depended on the efficiency of the code, how little CPU time could be used. Instructors taught us to value software efficiency. Hardware was too valuable to waste.

Today, these lessons are meaningless. A few years after graduation, we had minicomputers. PC's came next, then the internet, and more recently, mobile devices. I can think of no other technical advances that have the same broad impact on business processes.

I take it as a given there will be more change, and not just technology-driven change.

As a CEO, you can be a victim of change or lead change. You can disrupt others or others can disrupt you. You can grow your business or let competitors grow theirs. You can be satisfied with the profits you make or seek ways to improve.

In Chapter 24, I suggested ways to manage delegation and operational decision making in your marketing and sales process. Managing your personal time has benefits like more time for you, your family, or your personal pursuits. This is certainly a worthwhile way to spend it.

My primary motive, however, was to enable you time to manage the processes in your business.

Lead Change

Disrupt

Grow Your Business

Improve Your Profits

Or Be a Victim of Change

Be Disrupted

Let Competitor's Grow Their Business

Be Satisfied with Your Profits

FIGURE 38. You have a choice about which approach you should take with change.

What does a CEO do?

The process for managing the process is your duty as the leader of the business. On one hand, you want strong alignment and execution from your subordinates to keep your current marketing and sales processes humming.

This may sound contradictory at first, but you also want change to occur. This is how you can personally add value.

You should never consider your marketing and sales processes unchangeable and fixed. There are too many external forces.

Nor do you want a decision that prevents change in the future.

Lean thinking has a term for this, a monument. A monument is something in your business that could be costly to move or replace. It could be a family member difficult to fire. It could be a practice so ingrained you consider it culture. It could be a large, complex machine, or an expensive real estate investment.

When I worked for Maytag, I spent a lot of time in Maytag's Plant 2. This was a facility filled with monuments. There were big sheet metal presses; porcelain spray facilities and ovens; long, paced, and automated assembly lines; paint spray facilities and ovens; and automated storage and retrieval systems, just to name a few. Connecting these were eighteen miles of overhead monorail conveyors. About 50 percent of the workforce classified as indirect labor just to keep materials moving in the factory.

Another monument was the United Auto Workers. There were labor practices and work rules that could only change through contract negotiations. One reason for learning BQL was to assess payroll records to determine the frequency of the application of certain work rules so company negotiators could swap little-cost changes for big-savings changes in contract negotiations.

Companies with lots of monuments do not survive. Maytag did not survive.

A contrasting example is Herman Miller. Over the years, they have eschewed investments in factories with in-house parts manufacturing processes. Devoted to the latest design thinking, they view factory investments as being a barrier to design changes. Once you build a highly vertically integrated factory, you are later looking for ways to maximize the use of your investment.

In your marketing and sales process, you could have monuments. I see many companies with enterprise resource planning systems that do not work well for their marketing and sales teams. Changing these can be almost impossible once installed. Some companies see their commission plans as unchangeable. Others are fearful of approaching new channels of distribution, worrying those customers in existing channels will object.

High performing CEOs see this as an issue to manage. Whenever you buy, lease, contract, or put into practice a change, consider the exit plan for that change.

Managing Change is Your Business

If you are not watching, measuring, questioning, and advancing the processes in your business, who is?

If your competitor is changing faster than you, who will win in the market?

When you learn how to create a Business Model Canvas, you learn that pivoting is an important aspect. Your job is to validate all aspects of the model and act if the model is not functioning.

Sadly, I have met too many CEOs who try to put together a business model as a finished product, which it is not, as there are always changes in technology, moves by competition, and shifting end-user demand.

What should be changed next? is a better perspective for you to adopt than *What needs to be changed?*

Why Do CEOs Avoid Change?

Strategyzer suggests there are four forces involved in change[2].

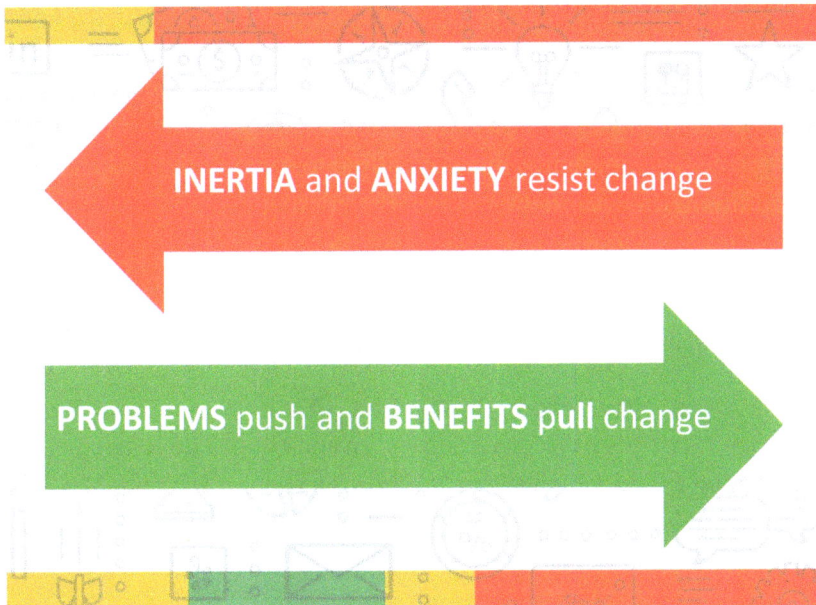

FIGURE 39. The dynamics of change.

The first two forces make changes difficult. The inertia of the current solution is a barrier to change. This includes the habits of the organization and the switching costs. Anxiety is another barrier. Novel solutions have a few unknowns, or you assume they have unknowns. Unknowns add risk and risk reduces the value of a proposed change.

The second two forces make change easier. Any problem, frustration, or pain point with an existing solution creates push for a new solution. The benefits or gains of a new solution create pull for the new ways to do things.

Resistance to change is nothing new. People must see or experience the benefits of change to support change.

I recall a situation my team once faced. We wanted to do business with a national wholesaler that had multiple warehouses and a catalog with a distribution of about three million copies.

The problem was a direct competitor was already in the catalog and the wholesaler had inventory in all their locations. They were willing to replace the competitor but not willing to carry both product lines. In addition, they wanted us to buy the competitive products, so they would not have a switching cost.

We had to think about this proposal. The competitive inventory had no value to us.

Nevertheless, we agreed to do the deal. To mitigate our expense, we took every item of the competitor's inventory and advertised it for sale in the city in which they were headquartered. We bought a full-page ad in the local newspaper and offered an 80 percent discount off the regular price.

We captured the customer, put our inventory in place in the warehouses, secured the catalog pages, added more catalog pages, and flooded the competitor's hometown market with deeply discounted products.

By expanding the offering in the catalog, if our competitor wanted to dispense payback, they faced a now-larger switching cost.

Another reason CEOs avoid change is their personality make-up. It is the personal stress and worry change causes them. Change comes with risk and there are only so many sleepless nights to worry about another change. If a CEO is averse to risk or looking to be a steadying influence on their organization, they may unintentionally be a barrier to change.

A CEO who has a detail-oriented personality may also spend time concerned with every aspect of a change and drag out the timeline.

My boss's-boss at Maytag, Dick, had this personality. It was frustrating to the point where my boss, Jim, refused to involve him unless necessary.

I was deeply involved in a project where this played out. We began to use computer simulation to model changes to the eighteen miles of conveyors in Maytag's Plant 2. Since these conveyors cost just over $1,300 per linear foot (2019 dollars), slight differences in design could make an enormous difference.

Our proposed modifications in this project saved about 600 feet or about $800,000 (2019 dollars).

Then word came down that my boss's-boss's-boss, Sterling, wanted to review what we proposed.

Uh-oh.

Dick was completely ignorant of what we were doing, and we had to tell him.

Dick had a gravelly voice, due to his affinity for Camel Straights. Typically, he punctuated his rants with occasional hissing sounds. A significant personality trait was his tendency to be over-the-top detail-oriented. He presented a confident outward demeanor but inwardly was very insecure.

Any project with his involvement took months to mature and implement. There was no limit to the amount of engineering which could go into a project if he was involved. Grass could grow faster than Dick could shepherd a project.

His first introduction to our work was twenty-four hours before the big meeting with Sterling. There was little Dick could do, but a lot he could say.

The highlight near the end of our disclosure began with a five second inhale between the teeth, a signature reaction for him, followed by snarling; "You ... guys ... had ... better ... be ... right." Dick's middle finger attacked the desktop with every word punctuating the points he wanted to make.

Of course, we were right. In addition, we prevailed in the big meeting with Sterling.

My boss was a fearless change-maker. In retrospect, I now see him as an unstoppable force that had to deal with an immovable object. Personalities matter.

I remember him for the confidence and courage he had to act independently.

I must note this occurred in the days when engineering was more about planning and less about experimentation. Before the popularity of lean thinking or lean start-up, management rewarded good engineers for good planning. One boss I had called it the *four P's*; proper planning prevents problems.

To that generation, the plans for escaping the Great Depression, the invasion of Normandy, and the development of the atomic bomb influenced the culture. Many of the business leaders of the era were veterans of World War II and previously served as officers in the military.

Change Justification

I worked for a company where there was a strong emphasis on cost reduction as justification for capital investment. There were written policies about the way a capital expenditure request was to be submitted and detailed forms for presenting financial calculations.

The engineers and accountants liked this process.

The CEO of the company, schooled to be an engineer, was the champion for the process. I understand why he insisted on uniformity, as it is difficult to consider alternative investment decisions if every proposal is prepared a separate way.

More recently, some companies have implemented practices where a Business Model Canvas goes with every investment proposal, including any proposed merger and acquisitions deal. This is a way to explain the comprehensive impact of an investment.

While the engineers and accountants liked the financial form-driven process, the CEO was the only one in the company who understood the forms that documented cost reduction were necessary but not enough to get his approval.

There was one specific project where a vice president and a group of manufacturing engineers worked several months on a specific project and put together a proposal for a major capital investment. The investment, about $3.6 million (2019 dollars), had less than a two-year payback.

They prepared drawings, asked for quotes, and outlined all the details of the project. There was no lack of financial documentation or champions for the project.

The CEO would not approve the investment even though the entire chain of command approved.

The justification used only financial cost reduction. The team did not bother to explore what the investment could do for new products, new markets, and shorter lead-times. In Business Model Canvas terms, they ignored most of the customer pains and gains.

The frustrated vice president and engineers shelved the project.

About ten years later, another vice president and some of the same engineers, proposed the same project (same facility, same product lines). One significant difference was this time the investment proposed was about $8 million (2019 dollars). The justification used cost reduction again.

Who said, "culture is easy to change?"

Another substantial difference in the project's resurrection was a new CEO, who was far less diligent, observant, and thoughtful than the previous CEO. He approved the project.

It failed miserably.

It was over-budget by the time it was completed. They discovered assumptions driving the math for savings were wrong and the return on investment was overstated. Furthermore, the specifications for the investment did not take into the account anything about trends in product mix or the needs for the order fulfillment processes.

A thinking CEO should not approve projects because the math is right.

Mentoring: Pay It Forward

This book began with a question. "Is your marketing and sales plan a person or a process?"

After reading every earlier chapter, you understand I am all-in for seeing it as a process. If you see it as a person, you are giving control to someone else of what could be the most important part of your business, especially a venture-funded start-up looking to scale.

You have other processes to manage in addition to marketing and sales. They will compete for your time; accounting, human resources, supply chain, order fulfillment, customer service, research and development, capital investment, agency approvals, ... just to name a few.

For some companies, the marketing and sales process is not the most important process.

However, you can ask the same question for the other processes; are they a person or a process? You already know my answer.

You will have to decide where to spend your time. Some processes are more broken than others are and need your attention.

You can single-handedly create competitive advantage if you manage your processes and changes to your processes better than your counterpart does at the competition.

What is next? If you are one of the few who manage to grow your business into an enterprise company, you will find yourself hiring general managers who manage processes for you. They may well be as unprepared as I was in 1988.

Hire those people you feel are a strong fit and coachable, then mentor them.

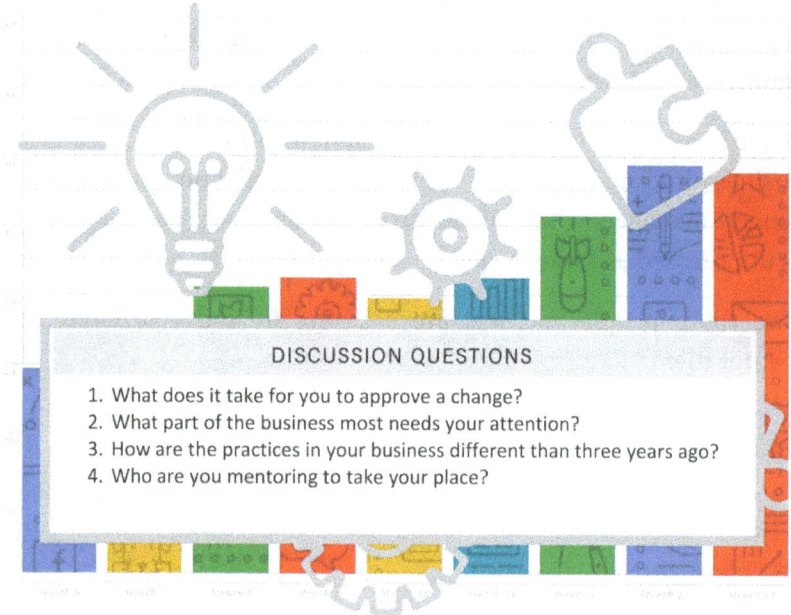

DISCUSSION QUESTIONS

1. What does it take for you to approve a change?
2. What part of the business most needs your attention?
3. How are the practices in your business different than three years ago?
4. Who are you mentoring to take your place?

28

THE FINAL PROCESS

N obody lives forever. Everybody exits his or her business. The way you exit can matter a lot, however. Some observers say there are only two ways you exit a business, voluntarily or involuntarily.

You have choices. You can have an exit where you pass the business to a relative, sell it to a key employee, sell it to a competitor, sell it to someone else, or simply shut it down. Shutting down the business may be your least attractive alternative. You get no value for what you built, employees lose jobs, and customers must find new sources for the products or services you provided.

Shutting down, unfortunately, is the fate for most small and medium-size businesses. By most estimates, 80 percent of the businesses that come for sale in America never sell.

Why Businesses Do Not Sell

Many small businesses do not generate enough cash. The owner takes a reasonable salary but builds little equity. In my work as a coach, this is typical for businesses with less than $1.5 million in revenues.

Why is cash flow important? When a sale of a small business is proposed, few individuals have the personal wealth to make much of an investment. If they seek financing, their lender will do diligence to explore how they could repay a loan.

If the cash generated by the business is only enough for a salary for the owner, the lender will decline to fund the deal. The only options for the seller are to gift the business to a relative, gift the business to an employee, or shut the business down.

Furthermore, in businesses with less than $1.5 million in revenues, an owner or partner is also likely to be the key salesperson in the business. This further complicates the deal.

If the owner is also the key sales person, a rational potential buyer doing diligence will discover the role played by the owner and have doubts about customer retention. Said another way, they will see added risk in the deal.

Whenever risk goes up, valuation goes down. If the concern is great enough, the buyer may move on to another opportunity.

Retaining the role as chief salesperson can also occur with larger businesses. To reduce the risk, a buyer might see with customer retention, the sales leader should be someone other than an owner, preferably a manager. This enables a new owner to step into the business in the same role as a seller, as a CEO who gives direction to the team.

One of the chronic issues in selling small businesses is the fact there are far more sellers than buyers. When your business is for sale, you are competing for buyers with owners of other businesses and businesses in other industries.

A useful way to assess your sales and marketing practices is to assess them in the context of the type of exit you want.

Five Levels for Exit Planning

When my clients and I discuss selling their small and medium-sized businesses, I use a rough framework to assess the possible exit plans they should consider. Most often, I can classify a business into one of five categories. With each category, the revenues of the business are different, the possible exit plan is different, and operational practices I expect to see are different.

If an exit plan is not urgent, I encourage the clients to look up to the next classification level and work to develop the performance and practices necessary to achieve a successful exit at the next level.

While there are exceptions, figure 40 explains my method for classification. I use revenues and cash flow as the first way to assess the business. The reason for this is due to the financing needs for a buyer.

Level I
 Revenues less than $500K-more a job than a business
 Adjusted cash flow typically less than $100K
 No exit likely

Level II
 Revenues from $500K to $2M
 Adjusted cash flow $100-200K
 Likely exit to a competitor

Level III
 Revenues from $2M to ~$7.5M
 Adjusted cash flow $200K to ~$750K
 Likely exit to family, competitor, or key employee

Level IV
 Revenues from ~$7.5M to ~$10M
 Adjusted cash flow ~$750 to ~$1M
 Exit to Private Equity buyer as a bolt-on acquisition

Level V
 Revenues greater than $10M
 Adjusted cash flow greater than $1M
 Exit to Private Equity buyer as a platform company

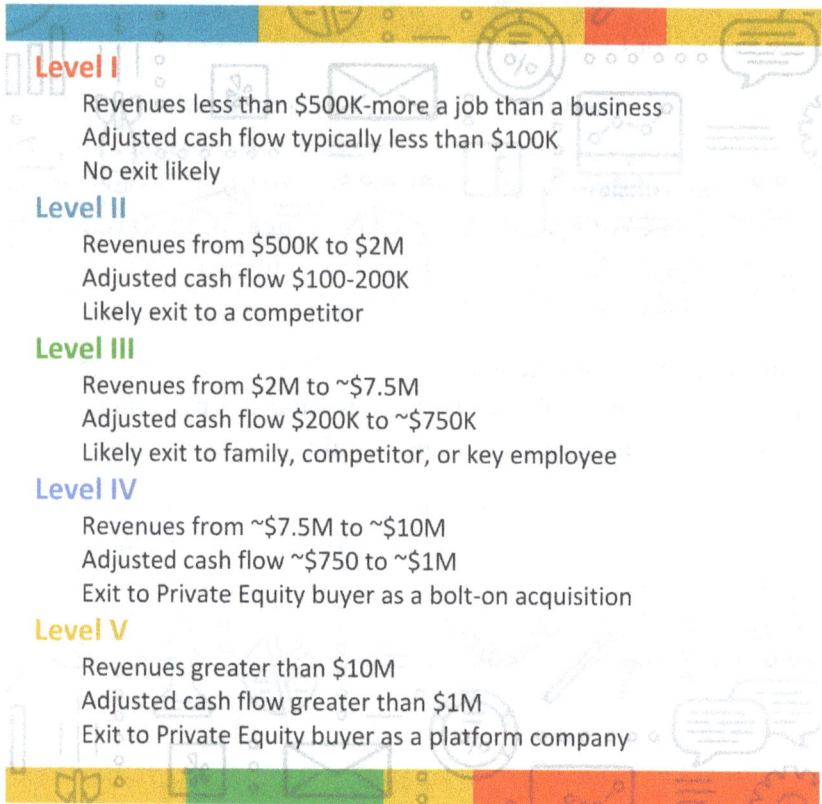

FIGURE 40. Classifications for exits.

Buyers can raise money several ways, but each type of investor or lender will insist on a return on their investment or repayment plan. This associates to the ability of the business to generate cash, which drives the valuation of the business.

Investments in inventory, real estate, equipment, and computers have no direct bearing on valuation. They are only important to the extent they enable cash flow from the business. Some sellers become emotional about this because they know what they paid or invested in these assets and see this as value.

In many businesses listed for sale, the pitch from the broker or investment banker patronizes this viewpoint. You might see a story like this, "This would be an excellent opportunity for someone with a sales or marketing background. Everything is in place to serve growth in the business." If they told the truth, the broker would note they have a client who has invested in capacity they do not need, inventory that does not turn enough, or a building/office that is too big.

If the financial profile of a business being sold is acceptable, buyers will do further diligence to assess the business to identify risks. What would they expect to find in sales and marketing practices in the business? Read on.

Sales and Marketing Expectations in Diligence

With Level I, there are little or no expectations. You can be employed and be independent. It is highly unlikely with this type of business that an exit is possible. Figure 41 suggests the typical practices seen in this kind of business.

Please note these practices are an observation, not a criticism. There are people with unusual or special talents that can share them with several customers. Examples might be certain types of doctors, attorneys or expert witnesses, special accounting services, or real estate agents. The specific talents of the individual are central to the business. You can have a successful career with this type of business.

Level I

Target Customer Segments usually not specified

Marketing messages are unclear or done at the discretion of the individual

No website, or a site not updated for four or more years

Business Owner is the Salesperson

No documented sales processes

No CRM

FIGURE 41. A level I business has little sophistication in practices.

A Level II business is one with a few employees or independent contractors. From my experience as a business coach, I see many businesses in this category. This type of business is where the CEOs put in long days, deal with issues personally, and suffer from stress.

The transition from a Level II business to a Level III business is difficult for many entrepreneurs. To succeed, the owner or CEO must move from working in the business to working on the business. Rather than doing things themselves, they must learn to hire, supervise, and delegate responsibilities to others.

For some, the reason they selected their business is a passion they had for the domain of their business. When you become a manager, you are no longer directly practicing your art. You use technical skills less and instead focus on supervision and management skills.

Some owners are reluctant to leave what they love. The consequence is usually a Level II business.

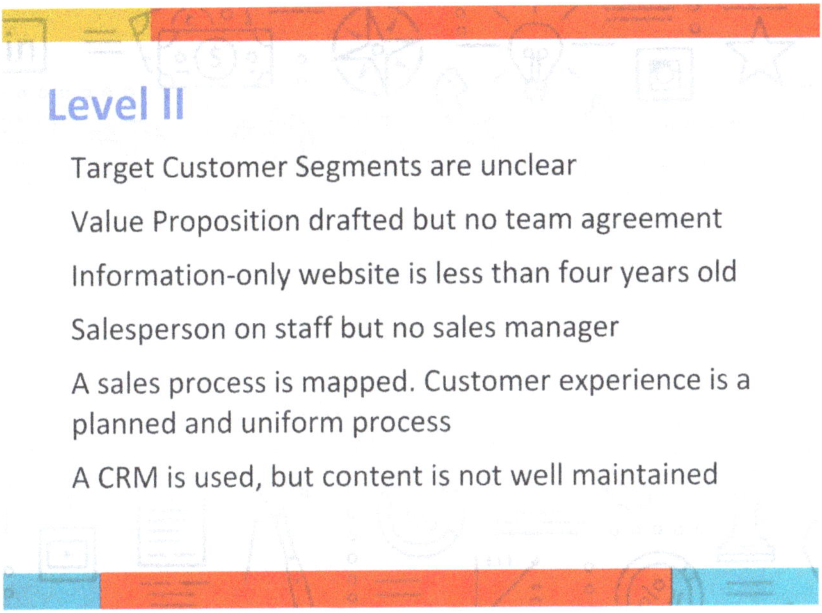

Level II

Target Customer Segments are unclear

Value Proposition drafted but no team agreement

Information-only website is less than four years old

Salesperson on staff but no sales manager

A sales process is mapped. Customer experience is a planned and uniform process

A CRM is used, but content is not well maintained

FIGURE 42. A level II business relies on the personal efforts of the CEO or owner.

Moreover, making the transition from Level II to Level III increases the chances for a profitable sale of the business. When an owner has a key role in the operation of the business, a new buyer must replace the critical role when the seller exits. This raises risk and lowers valuation.

Suppose the seller was the chief sales and marketing person for the business. A rational buyer will note the role of the seller. If they are not comfortable assuming the role or know they are not suited for the role, they will walk from the deal, or offer significantly less than a seller might want.

This is not an issue where you should try to spin your situation in the way you sell the business. In many business sales, a revenue earn-out is part of the way a deal is structured. An earn-out provides some of the proceeds of the sale contingent on future revenues of the business.

Level III

The target customer segment has clear definition

There is a clear value proposition

The website includes a regularly updated blog

A sales manager leads the sales team

There is a lead generation process

Sales progress is tracked in a CRM

FIGURE 43. In a level III business, you implement practices through orders.

Any earn-out carries certain risks, as future performance of the business is not just dependent on the current team and current practices of the business. It also depends on what the new owner does with the business. Some advisors suggest earn-outs have no value at all to the seller.

However, if you accept an earn-out as part of the structure of the sale, you should do it, in part, because you have some confidence the business can grow without you.

A Level IV or Level V business is one that might appeal to a private equity buyer who is trying to build and sell a bigger business to a public buyer or to a larger private entity. Some will refer to Level IV businesses as middle-market businesses. The goal for a private equity buyer is to build a company typically bigger than $50 million with a tight strategic focus.

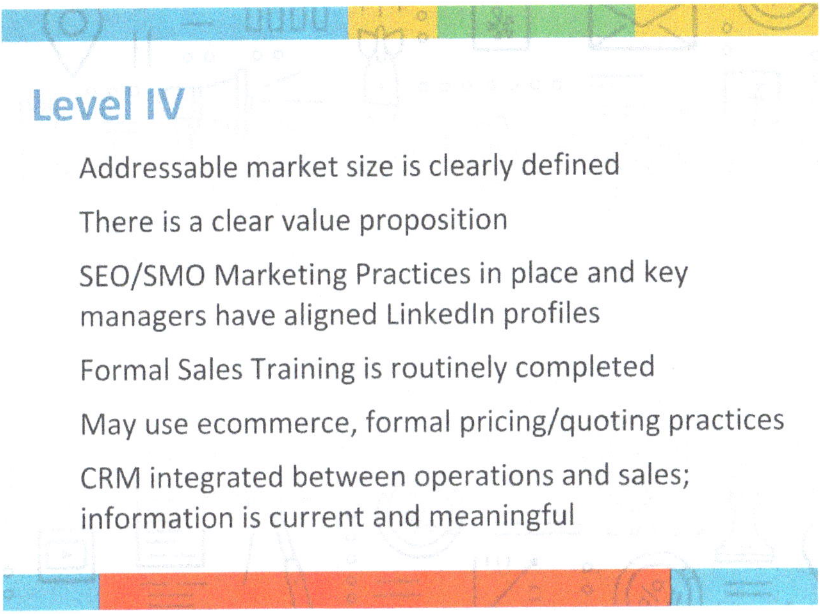

Level IV

Addressable market size is clearly defined

There is a clear value proposition

SEO/SMO Marketing Practices in place and key managers have aligned LinkedIn profiles

Formal Sales Training is routinely completed

May use ecommerce, formal pricing/quoting practices

CRM integrated between operations and sales; information is current and meaningful

FIGURE 44. Moving from level III to IV is usually a matter of scaling the business.

For an owner to move from a Level III to a Level IV business, usually the greatest challenge involves scaling the business; more customers, more salespeople, and more revenues.

A Level V business is one that can be a platform business. This is a business where the practices inside the business can serve as the template or platform used when they buy other businesses. A Level IV business is a strong fit to the platform business but lacks the scale and operational strengths of the Level V business. Some people in the private equity business refer to the Level IV business as a bolt-on business.

A Level V business is typically the best possible outcome for an exiting-owner. Buyers consider these businesses the top performers in their industry. It is usually obvious that there are internal practices to implement into bolt-on acquisitions.

Level V

Addressable market is clearly growing

Value Proposition is clearly defined and articulated

Content is actively managed on all relevant websites and social media

Company salespeople are best in the industry

More than 30% of leads result in sales

CRM maintenance is considered an integral part of the business

FIGURE 45. Key processes in a level V business.

Level V businesses attract a high multiple because they are necessary to begin a project where the aim is growth through acquisition. Buying a series of businesses with bad practices only creates a larger business with bad practices.

Looking Up

No matter what level your business is in today, you have an opportunity to move up if you give yourself enough time.

The valuation of your business is not a metric important to most employees unless they are shareholders. Those concerned will be a small group.

How much time is necessary?

If you allow less than a year to work on your business, your chances of reaching another level might not be that great. Most experts suggest three to five years might be the best horizon to consider when you are creating an exit plan.

Even that horizon might be a challenge if you consume your available hours with day-to-day activities in the business. You can best address exit planning when you are working *on* the business, not *in* the business.

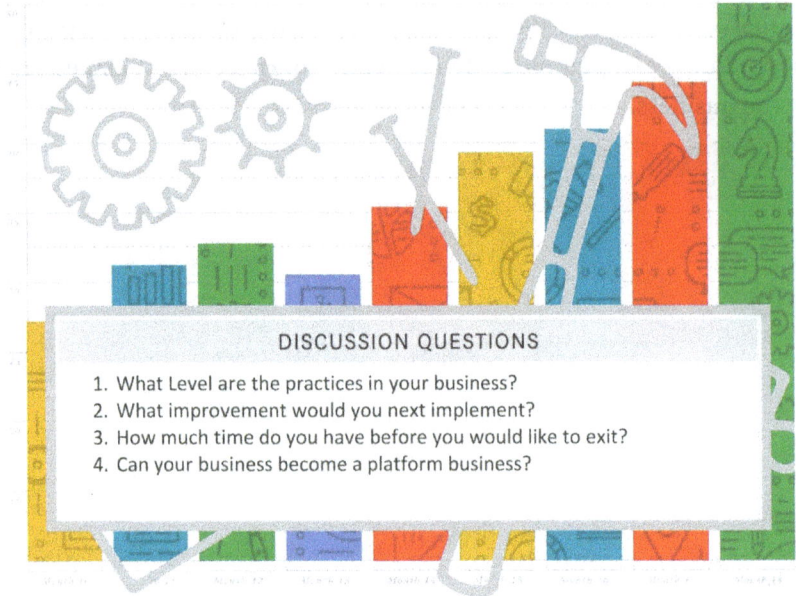

DISCUSSION QUESTIONS

1. What Level are the practices in your business?
2. What improvement would you next implement?
3. How much time do you have before you would like to exit?
4. Can your business become a platform business?

NOTES

1. A Person or a Process?

1. Ronald Reagan, Speaking My Mind: Selected Speeches (New York: Simon and Schuster, 2004).
2. https://en.wikipedia.org/wiki/W._Edwards_Deming

4. Strong Fit, Weak Interest

1. https://www.bni.com/

5. Buying Determinants

1. Ronald Kessler, "GSA Stops Furniture Purchases," The Washington Post (October 11, 1979). https://www.washingtonpost.com/archive/politics/1979/10/11/gsa-stops-furniture-purchases/aae5e218-830b-49e7-aa8d-fe57471d1ffa/?noredirect=on&utm_term=.7a5417d29774
2. https://www.wework.com/

8. A Cost you Can Influence

1. https://www.yelp.com/
2. https://www.glassdoor.com/index.htm
3. https://www.linkedin.com/
4. https://www.facebook.com/

9. Ten Audiences Which Matter

1. https://en.wikipedia.org/wiki/Maytag#Ol'_Lonely

10. Customer Experience

1. https://www.glassdoor.com/index.htm
2. https://www.google.com/business/?ppsrc=GPDA2

12. Challenging Your Customers

1. Matthew Dixon and Brent Adamson, The Challenger Sale (New York: Portfolio Penguin, 2011).
2. Dixon and Adamson, *Challenger Sale*, xiv.
3. Dixon and Adamson, *Challenger Sale*, 22.
4. Dixon and Adamson, *Challenger Sale*, 12.
5. LinkedIn Sales Solutions, "How B2B Buyers Perceive Sales Professionals." https://business.linkedin.com/sales-solutions/blog/h/how-b2b-buyers-perceive-sales-professionals.

13. Is Patience A Virtue?

1. Dixon and Adamson, *Challenger Sale*, 185.

14. The Right Tool For The Job

1. Dixon and Adamson, *Challenger Sale*, 141.
2. https://www.strategyzer.com/
3. https://www.pxtselect.com/Home.aspx
4. https://www.criteriacorp.com/
5. https://www.smoothhiring.com/
6. https://www.discprofile.com/
7. https://www.myersbriggs.org/my-mbti-personality-type/mbti-basics/home.htm?bhcp=1

15. A Challenge For The Leader

1. Dixon and Adamson, *Challenger Sale*, xiv.
2. Global Leadership Network, "Wise, Foolish or Evil: Which One Are You Going to Be?" https://globalleadership.org/articles/leading-others/wise-foolish-evil-one-going-dr-henry-cloud/.

16. Leaders Need Followers

1. David Hoffeld, The Science of Selling: Proven Strategies to Make Your Pitch, Influence Decisions, and Close the Deal (New York: Tarcher Perigee, 2016).
2. https://blog.hubspot.com/sales/best-sales-training-programs

18. Comfort Is The Lack Of Discomfort

1. https://www.whatissixsigma.net/pareto-chart-and-analysis/

20. The Case For Spending On Marketing

1. https://ads.google.com/intl/en_ca/home/
2. https://www.facebook.com/business

21. Connect And Compete

1. Salesforce, State of Marketing Report, 5th ed., 3.

23. Seven Wastes In Marketing And Sales

1. https://www.strategyzer.com/
2. https://www.strategyzer.com/canvas/business-model-canvas
3. https://www.strategyzer.com/canvas/value-proposition-canvas

24. What Could Possibly Go Wrong?

1. Chris O'Brien, "Uber Has Reportedly Been Sued at Least 433 times in 2017," *VentureBeat*, (August 24, 2017) https://venturebeat.com/2017/08/23/uber-has-reportedly-been-sued-at-least-433-times-in-2017/.

26. Grease The Squeaky Wheel

1. William Oncken and Donald L. Wass, "Management Time: Who's Got the Monkey?" Harvard Business Review (November/December 1999). https://hbr.org/1999/11/management-time-whos-got-the-monkey.

27. The Process For Managing The Process

1. https://en.wikipedia.org/wiki/Moore%27s_law
2. Alexander Osterwalder, "How Customers Adopt Products" *Strategyzer* (September 11, 2017). https://blog.strategyzer.com/posts/2017/9/11/how-customers-adopt-products.

www.ingramcontent.com/pod-product-compliance
Lightning Source LLC
Chambersburg PA
CBHW071203210326
41597CB00016B/1654